I0003243

POWERSHELL TUTORIAL VOLUME 1:

7 Practical Tutorials That Will Get You Scripting In No Time

By Victor Ashiedu

VICTOR ASHIEDU

INTRODUCTION

I want to thank you and congratulate you for buying the book, *"PowerShell Tutorial, Volume 1: 7 Practical Tutorials That Will Get You Scripting In No Time"*.

Why is this book different? It is hands-on! That is the simple answer. After the content page, there is a guide on how to download and install the lab you require to read this book.

From the many feedbacks I have received from colleagues and my online collaboration, many Windows Sys Admins would love to learn PowerShell. The challenge is they simply do not know where to start. If this statement describes your thoughts, you are not alone; but you have the solution right in your hands!

If you thought learning PowerShell was very difficult, then think again! *"PowerShell Tutorial, Volume 1"* is the first of this book series that brings PowerShell skills to your fingertips. It simplifies and shortens the process of learning Windows PowerShell.

"PowerShell Tutorial, Volume 1" starts by introducing you to cmdlets. It then teaches you how to find cmdlets using the Get-Command cmdlet. Next, you will learn how to use the Get-Help cmdlet to find help. By the time you finish this volume, you would have starting scripting.

"PowerShell Tutorial, Volume 1" is structured in a way that teaches you PowerShell skills in a sequence. What's more, you will execute commands and build scripts as you read. Welcome to PowerShell!

Thanks again for buying this book, I hope you enjoy it!

COPYRIGHT AND DISCLAIMER

and the publication of the trademark is without permission or backing by the trademark owners.

Print copy ISBN information

ISBN-10: 1519548907

ISBN-13: 978-1519548900

DEDICATION

To my late dad, Mr. Lawrence Ashiedu and my mum, Mrs. Philomena Ashiedu

Table of Contents

DOWNLOAD AND INSTALL YOUR LAB FOR THIS BOOK

Lab Requirements

To be able to install the lab successfully, you will need the following:

1. A desktop PC or Laptop with Intel VT or AMD-V virtualization hardware.
2. Physical memory install - Minimum 6GB, recommended 8GB (more is better!).
3. Windows 8.1 or Windows 10 Professional or Enterprise.
4. At least 10GB available space on a partition on the computer.
5. Microsoft account (Live, Hotmail, etc).

How to Download the Lab

The Lab for "PowerShell Tutorial" book series can be downloaded from the link below:

https://gallery.technet.microsoft.com/scriptcenter/PowerShell-Tutorial-Script-09b38b97

After downloading the zip file, follow the steps below to install the Lab:
1. Unzip the downloaded PSLab.zip file.
2. Copy PSLab folder to the root of your preferred drive.
3. Locate the text file called 'PSLab Install Guide v3.0' in <DriveName>:\PSLab\Tools\PSLab_Scripts.   Where <DriveName> is the drive you copied PSLab folder in step 2.
4. Follow the instruction in 'PSLab Install Guide v3.0' to install the lab.

Important information about the Lab

1. Ensure that you enable Intel VT or AMD-V virtualization hardware extensions in the BIOS.
2. Lab installation is fully automated and should take approximately 45 minutes to complete.
3. After installing the lab, you will have a Virtual Server called PSLabSRV with IP address 10.0.0.2
4. PSLabSRV is a domain controller in the PSLab.Local domain.
5. You will require this domain controller for any command relating to Active Directory within this book.
6. Windows 8.1 or Windows 10 Professional or Enterprise has Hyper-V capabilities. Hyper-V is enabled as part of the lab installation.
7. The lab in this Tutorial was tested on Windows 8.1 Professional, Windows 8.1 Enterprise and Windows 10 Professional.
8. Once you have installed the lab, you can use it for the entire "PowerShell Tutorial" book series.

Important information about commands and images shown in this book

1. In parts of this book, images of results of commands have been shown. This is to give the reader something to compare to.
2. The images are for illustrations purposes only and is not intended to replace the need for the reader to run the commands themselves.
3. Running the commands in this book is part of the learning objective. The reader is strongly encouraged to run the commands.
4. Images in this book have been optimized as much as possible. If you are reading the Kindle version of this book, you may zoom the images to get a proper view.

POWERSHELL TUTORIAL
1
Introduction to PowerShell and cmdlets

PowerShell is a command line tool used for task automation. In my opinion, Windows PowerShell is one of the greatest tools built by Microsoft in recent years.

In this first tutorial, I will introduce you to PowerShell. For readers new to PowerShell, the first section of this tutorial will act as a quick introduction to this exciting tool. For readers that have some knowledge of PowerShell, it will act as a refresher. There is something for every reader in this tutorial. I encourage you to read every page.

This tutorial also covers PowerShell cmdlets (Command-Lets) and shows you how to find cmdlets using the Get-Command cmdlet. The tutorial covers cmdlets in details including how they are named in Verb-Noun pairs. The tutorial concludes by teaching you cmdlet parameters and aliases as well as the command completion capability of PowerShell.

Topics covered in this tutorial will be treated under the following headings:

1.0 What is PowerShell?

1.1 Introduction to cmdlets

1.2 Cmdlet Parameters, Aliases and Command Completion

1.3 How To Find Cmdlets Using Get-Command

1.4 How To Use 'Verb' and 'Noun' Parameters of Get-Command

1.0 What is PowerShell?

Wikipedia defines Windows PowerShell as "a task automation and configuration management framework". Microsoft defines it as "a new Windows command-line shell designed especially for system administrators".

I define Windows PowerShell as a command-line and scripting tool built for Windows Systems Administrators for the purpose of Windows task automation.

For a newbie reading this book, one way to easily introduce PowerShell is to relate it to the Windows command prompt. Relating Windows PowerShell to the legacy Windows command prompt somehow undermines PowerShell but it is a way to easily relate PowerShell to you.

Working with Windows PowerShell

As this book is a hands-on book, I am going to dive straight into the real thing. To access Windows PowerShell command line tool, search for "Windows PowerShell" and click on it.

Note
To open PowerShell on Windows 8.1, click the Windows logo and search for "Windows PowerShell". For Windows 10 users, simply enter "Windows PowerShell" on the search box in the task bar.

As you can see, the PowerShell command console is very similar to the legacy Windows command prompt. But there is more to it.

I guess the next logical thing you want to do is start executing PowerShell commands! Not yet. Let me get some minor but important things out of the way first.

Like most applications, PowerShell comes in different versions. It is important that you know the version of PowerShell you are running. It is also important to know how to upgrade Windows PowerShell if you need to.

There are two ways to determine your current PowerShell version. By executing either of the commands below:

```
$PSVersionTable
```

Or

```
Get-Host
```

The preferred command is $PSVersionTable. See Figure 1.0.0 for details. Although there is a number of information from the results of the commands, I will concentrate on "PSVersion" from the first command and "Version" from the second command.

As at the time of writing, the latest available PowerShell version is 5.0. Your PowerShell version should be at least 4.0 (Windows 8.1), I strongly recommend that you upgrade to version 5.0. Upgrading your PowerShell version simply requires you to install the Windows Management Framework (WMF) for the version of PowerShell you wish to upgrade to.

I have included a download link to Windows "Management Framework 5.0 Preview April 2015" at the end of Tutorial 1. This is the WMF for PowerShell 5.0.

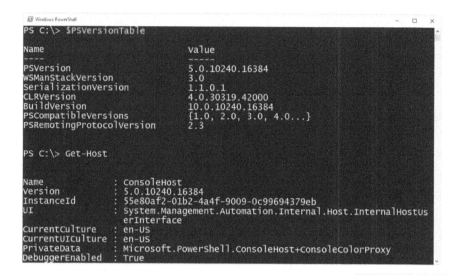

Figure 1.0.0 - $PSVersionTable or Get-Host command

Section Summary

In this section we covered the following:

1. Introduced Windows PowerShell as a command-line and scripting tool built for Windows Systems Administrators for the purpose of Windows task automation.
2. Learnt how to access Windows PowerShell on your computer
3. Learnt how to check the PowerShell version installed on your computer by executing the *$PSVersionTable* or *Get-Host* command.

1.1 Introduction To Cmdlets

Windows PowerShell executes commands using cmdlets (Command-Lets). Cmdlet is an entirely new concept introduced with PowerShell. They are command-line tools built into the shell in PowerShell.

Cmdlets are normally made of two words. The first word is a verb, while the second is a noun. A cmdlet Verb and its Noun are separated with a hyphen(-). A cmdlet is named in Verb-Noun pairs.

The verb part of a cmdlet is usually an action word while the Noun part is the identity on which the action is performed. For example Get-Command. The Verb part of this cmdlet is 'Get' while the Noun part (the object on which the 'Get' action is performed) is 'Command'. This is the standard naming convention of cmdlets.

Even though PowerShell uses the verb part of a cmdlet to imply an action, the word may not necessarily be a standard English verb. For example the word 'New' is a PowerShell verb but it is not an English verb.

Note

Windows PowerShell cmdlets are named in Verb-Noun pairs. The Verb portion identifies the action to be performed while the Noun portion identifies the entity on which that action is performed. PowerShell verbs may not necessarily be English Language verbs.

Another important thing to note about cmdlets is that the Verb-Noun combination are usually descriptive of what the cmdlet accomplishes. An example of a cmdlet is Get-Help. This, like most PowerShell cmdlets is descriptive of what it does. Get-Help means get help! Our previous example, Get-Command, gets information about other PowerShell commands or cmdlets. Get-Command is clearly descriptive.

To drive my point home, let's examine some PowerShell verbs and see the reasoning behind them. The verb 'Add' adds a resource to a container. For example the cmdlet Add-Content, adds additional information to a file. The verb 'Set' is used to replace an existing data. For example, to amend the details of an Active Directory user, you would use the cmdlet Set-ADUser. This consistency in cmdlet names makes it easy to learn.

The examples below illustrates the points in the preceding paragraphs. To create a new file and send the data in the console to the file, execute the command below in your PowerShell console:

```
"This is the first line in the text file Outfile.txt" | Out-File
"<DriveName>:\PSLab\Tutorial 1\Outfile.txt"
```

Note

In the previous command, change 'DriveName' to the drive you copied PSLab folder to when you installed the lab. For the rest part of this series, anywhere you see 'DriveName' in a command, always replace it with your drive letter.

POWERSHELL TUTORIAL VOLUME 1

I used pipeline (|) in the example above. I will cover this concept and its usage in Tutorial 3.4.

As you can see from the example, a file is created in the path specified with the information *This is the first line in the text file Outfile.txt*. To add additional data into the text file without deleting the original data, execute the command below:

```
"This is the second line in the text file Outfile.txt" | Add-Content "<DriveName>:\PSLab\Tutorial 1\Outfile.txt"
```

The command above will add the information *This is the second line in the text file Outfile.txt* to the file Outfile.txt. As you may have guessed, this is not the only way to append data to a text file. Using Out-File with the -append parameter will accomplish the same task. These examples were meant to illustrate the workings of PowerShell cmdlets.

Add-Content or Out-File (with the -append parameter) cmdlets can be very useful when appending data to a text file and do not want to over-write the previous data on the text file.

Note

To illustrate PowerShell Verb-Noun format, note the following verbs and what they accomplish - the verb 'Add', adds a resource to a container, 'Set' is used to replace an existing data, while 'Get' verb specifies an action that retrieves a resource. Further reading can be found in Reference 1 at the end of the Tutorial 1.

Reserved PowerShell Words

In Windows PowerShell, some words have special meaning. These words are referred to as "Reserved Words". When you use any of these words in scripts without quotation marks, Windows PowerShell attempts to apply the special meaning assigned to the word.

Some of the reserved words in PowerShell are "Function", "Try", "Catch", "If", "Else", "ElseIf", "Break", "ForEach" and "In". For a full list of reserved words, see Reference 5 at the end of Tutorial 1.

I intentionally introduced these reserved words early in this tutorial because we will be using a number of them as we progress. If you wish to get information about any of these reserved words, execute the command "Get-Help about_ReservedWord". For example, to get information about "ForEach", execute the command below:

Get-Help about_ForEach

A portion of the result of above command is shown in Figure 1.1.0.

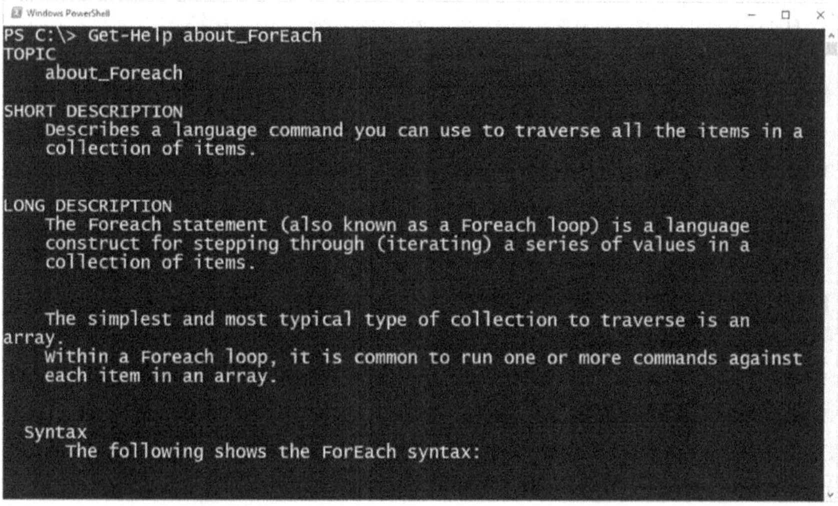

Figure 1.1.0 - Get-Help about_ForEach

Tutorial 2 covers the Get-Help command. It will also cover PowerShell "Windows PowerShell Core About Topics". In Tutorial 2, you will learn a lot more about how to find information about PowerShell reserved words using the Get-Help.

Section Summary

In this section we covered the following:

1. Windows PowerShell executes commands using cmdlets (Command-Lets).
2. Cmdlets are at the heart of PowerShell and are named in Verb-Noun pairs.
3. The Verb portion of a cmdlet identifies an action to be performed while the Noun portion identifies the entity on which that action is performed.
4. Windows PowerShell has some words with special meanings. They are called 'Reserved Words'.
5. If a reserved word is executed without a quotation mark, Windows PowerShell attempts to apply the special meaning assigned to the word.

1.2 Cmdlet Parameters, Aliases and Command Completion

We have already seen that PowerShell cmdlets are named in Verb-Noun pairs. In this section, I will introduce another important cmdlet concept called parameters. A cmdlet parameter is "the mechanism that allows a cmdlet to accept input". It simply means that a parameter allows you to feed information into a cmdlet.

Syntax of a Cmdlet Parameter

In this book, you will meet the word 'Syntax' several times. A PowerShell command syntax tells you the correct way to execute commands using a PowerShell cmdlet.

Below is the syntax of a cmdlet parameter:

```
Cmdlet_Name -ParameterName Parameter-Value
```

In the syntax example above, 'Cmdlet_Name' represents a cmdlet. The parameter name comes after the cmdlet preceded by a hyphen (-), followed by the parameter value.

For example, the Get-Command cmdlet has a parameter called Name. If I want to check whether a cmdlet called Get-Process is installed on my system, I will execute the command below:

```
Get-Command -Name Get-Process
```

In the previous command, 'Get-Command' is the cmdlet, 'Name' is the parameter name while 'Get-Process' is the parameter value. In this example, the 'Name' parameter has provided a way for me to feed input into the Get-Command cmdlet.

Note

A parameter allows a cmdlet to accept inputs. A cmdlet will normally have a number of parameters. A parameter usually come after a cmdlet followed by the value of the parameter.

If a cmdlet parameter allows me to feed input into the cmdlet, it means I can feed in different inputs into the same cmdlet to get different results. Earlier, we fed in 'Get-Process' into the 'Name' parameter of the Get-Command cmdlet.

We will now feed in a different value. Say we want to check whether the cmdlet Get-WMIObject is on my PC, Get-WMIObject will then replace Get-Process as my parameter value as shown below:

```
Get-Command -Name Get-WMIObject
```

Exciting! We have a different result by varying the parameter of the same cmdlet. See Figure 1.2.0.

```
Windows PowerShell                                          —  □  ×
PS C:\> Get-Command -Name Get-Process

CommandType        Name                                   Version
-----------        ----                                   -------
Cmdlet             Get-Process                            3.1.0.0

PS C:\> Get-Command -Name Get-WMIObject

CommandType        Name                                   Version
-----------        ----                                   -------
Cmdlet             Get-WmiObject                          3.1.0.0

PS C:\>
```

Figure 1.2.0 - Cmdlet Parameters (Same cmdlet, different results)

Types of Parameters

Some cmdlet parameters will accept input values, others will not. The parameters that accept input values are called 'Strings'. The parameters that do not accept input values are called 'switches'.

We have seen a parameter that accepts or requires inputs. An example of a parameter that do not require any input value is the 'Recurse' parameter found in the Get-ChildItem cmdlet.

The Get-ChildItem cmdlet displays the items and child items in one or more specified locations. If the item in question is a container (a folder for example), Get-ChildItem retrieves the items inside the container. The items inside the container are known as child items.

By default Get-ChildItem retrieves only items in the main container. If you wish to retrieve information about items in all child containers, use the 'Recurse' parameter. I have the folder structure below on my computer:

Name	Date modified	Type
1.0	14-Sep-15 22:11	File folder
1.1	15-Sep-15 21:46	File folder
1.2	15-Sep-15 21:37	File folder
1.3	15-Sep-15 21:38	File folder

Figure 1.2.1 - Parameter switche example with Get-ChildItem (folder structure)

Let's see the result of executing the following command:

Get-ChildItem "E:\Google Drive\Books\PowerShell Books\New 2015\Volume 1\Images\Tutorial 1"

```
PS C:\> Get-ChildItem "E:\Google Drive\Books\PowerShell Books\New 2015\Volume
1\Images\Tutorial 1"


    Directory: E:\Google Drive\Books\PowerShell Books\New 2015\Volume
    1\Images\Tutorial 1


Mode                LastWriteTime         Length Name
----                -------------         ------ ----
d-----        07-Nov-15     11:42                1.0
d-----        07-Nov-15     11:45                1.1
d-----        07-Nov-15     11:52                1.2
d-----        09-Oct-15     22:13                1.3
d-----        09-Oct-15     22:20                1.4


PS C:\>
```

Figure 1.2.2 - Parameter switche example with Get-ChildItem (Command without 'Recurse' parameter)

Now see what happens when you execute the same command with the 'Recurse' parameter. Notice that the 'Recurse' parameter does not have any input value. Compare this to the 'Name' parameter used in the Get-Command cmdlet earlier.

> Get-ChildItem -Recurse "E:\Google
> Drive\Books\PowerShell Books\New 2015\Volume
> 1\Images\Tutorial 1"

```
    Directory: E:\Google Drive\Books\PowerShell Books\New 2015\Volume
    1\Images\Tutorial 1\1.0

Mode                LastWriteTime         Length Name
----                -------------         ------ ----
-a----        07-Nov-15     11:38         260396 Figure-1.0.0.jpeg

    Directory: E:\Google Drive\Books\PowerShell Books\New 2015\Volume
    1\Images\Tutorial 1\1.1

Mode                LastWriteTime         Length Name
----                -------------         ------ ----
-a----        09-Oct-15     21:41         141631 Figure 1.1.0 - Get-Help
                                                 about_ForEach.jpeg
-a----        07-Nov-15     11:45         243576 Figure 1.1.0.jpeg

    Directory: E:\Google Drive\Books\PowerShell Books\New 2015\Volume
    1\Images\Tutorial 1\1.2
```

Figure 1.2.3 - Parameter switche example with Get-ChildItem (Command with 'Recurse' parameter) - Some results not shown.

Using the Recurse parameter displays information about directories and subdirectories.

PowerShell Command Completion

Another important thing to note about PowerShell is its command completion functionality. Command completion is very useful as you then do not need to know a command in full in order to use it.

Command completion functionality of PowerShell provides it with the ability to auto complete commands for you. When you type a portion of a cmdlet and press the tab key, the shell completes the command for you. Command completion can be used for cmdlets as well as parameter completion.

For example, assuming you wish to find the Get-Command cmdlet but you have forgotten the full name of the cmdlet. You could type Get-Co then hit the tab key. Based on the commands I have on my system, the shell returned Get-Command, Get-ComputerRestorePoint, Get-Content, etc. As you press the tab key, the shell will return more and more cmdlets.

With this functionality, you do not need to memorize cmdlets - though as you script more and more you get used to some cmdlets, but command completion will remain useful in your scripting life!

Continuing with our Get-Command example, once you have found the cmdlet using command completion, you may wish to find the parameters associated with the cmdlet. To achieve this, simply hit the SHIFT key and type hyphen (-). Then press the Tab key once more. Continue pressing the tab key to see all parameters associated with the cmdlet (in this instance, Get-Command).

You may also press the SHIFT key and type hyphen (-) then press the tab key for the next parameter. See Figures 1.0.4 for illustration. We will cover parameters in much more details in the next section.

Figure 1.2.4 - Parameter - Command Completion

PowerShell Cmdlet Aliases

The last two useful functionalities in PowerShell that I wish to introduce to you are aliases, high-light-to-copy and right-click-to-paste. Most PowerShell cmdlets will have an alias. Aliases are alternate names for cmdlets and commands. They are usually shortened form of a cmdlet.

An alias in PowerShell is an alternate name or nickname for a cmdlet or for a command element, such as a function, script, file, or executable file. Most people use aliases in commands and scripts to reduce the number of letters they type. Aliases might also be easier to remember.

I personally like to use the full name of a cmdlet as it easy to recognize what the cmdlet does rather than trying to figure out the full name of an alias. This is my personal preference which you don't have to adopt.

You can get information about all cmdlet aliases on your computer by typing...can you guess? You guessed right, Get-Alias! When I executed Get-Alias on my PowerShell console, it returned what is shown in Figure 1.2.5. To see aliases available in your computer, execute the command:

```
Get-Alias | More
```

If you know an Alias and wish to find the full name of the cmdlet, you can execute:

```
Get-Alias -Name Alias_Name
```

For example, the alias for Get-WmiObject is gwmi. To find the full cmdlet for gwmi, execute the command:

```
Get-Alias -Name gwmi
```

To find the cmdlet with the alias ? (Yes ?), execute the command:

```
Get-Alias -Name ?
```

You may also use a wild-card, for example *Get-Alias -Name gw** as shown below.

```
Get-Alias -Name gw*
```

Result is shown in Figure 1.2.6 (the second command).

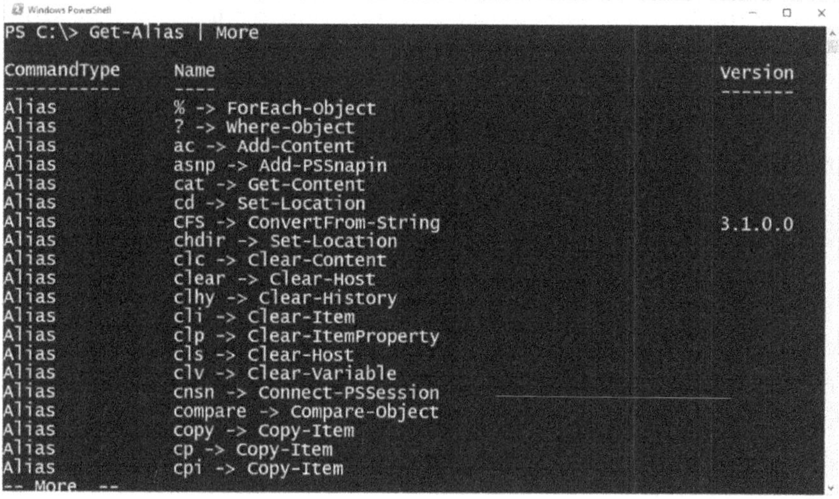

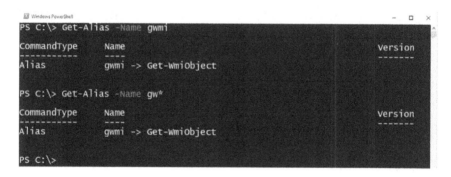

Figure 1.2.5 - Get-Alias

Figure 1.2.6 - Get-Alias gwmi

Note

Most PowerShell cmdlets have aliases. Aliases are alternate names for cmdlets and commands. They are usually shortened form of a cmdlet. You can use cmdlet aliases in place of the cmdlet.

Finally, let me introduce another brilliant feature of PowerShell. PowerShell pastes what is copied in your clipboard into the console when you right-clicking the PowerShell console. This can be very useful as it reduces your typing.

You can also copy an item from the console by simply highlighting it and hitting the Enter key. To illustrate this, highlight Get-WmiObject from the result of Figure 1.2.6 and hit the Enter key. To paste what you copied, simply right-click the console. See Figure 1.2.7 for illustration.

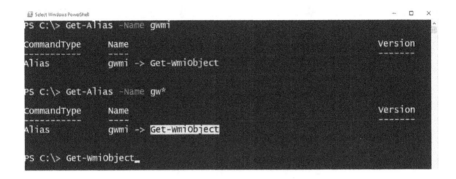

Figure 1.2.7 - Copy and Paste in a Shell

Section Summary

In this section we covered the following:

1. A cmdlet parameter is "the mechanism that allows a cmdlet to accept input".
2. The syntax of a cmdlet parameter is:
   Cmdlet_Name -ParameterName Parameter-Value
3. There are two types of parameters: 'Strings' and 'switches'. The 'String' parameter types accept input values while the 'switche' parameter types do not accept input values.
4. PowerShell supports command and parameter completion using the tab key. To use this functionality, enter a portion of the command and press the tab key. PowerShell automatically suggests commands based on your entry.
5. In Windows PowerShell, An alias is an alternate name or nickname for a cmdlet or for a command element, such as a function, script, file, or executable file.

1.3 How To Find Cmdlets Using Get-Command

Open a PowerShell console and execute the command below:

```
Get-Command | more
```

You should have a list of information displayed in your console. It should be similar to Figure 1.3.0 below.

```
Windows PowerShell                                                    —   □   ×
PS C:\> Get-Command | more

CommandType     Name                                           Version
-----------     ----                                           -------
Alias           Add-ProvisionedAppxPackage                     3.0
Alias           Add-VMToCluster                                2.0.0.0
Alias           Add-WindowsFeature                             2.0.0.0
Alias           Apply-WindowsUnattend                          3.0
Alias           Disable-ClusterS2D                             2.0.0.0
Alias           Disable-PhysicalDiskIndication                 2.0.0.0
Alias           Disable-StorageDiagnosticLog                   2.0.0.0
Alias           Enable-ClusterS2D                              2.0.0.0
Alias           Enable-PhysicalDiskIndication                  2.0.0.0
Alias           Enable-StorageDiagnosticLog                    2.0.0.0
Alias           Expand-IscsiVirtualDisk                        2.0.0.0
Alias           Export-DnsServerTrustAnchor                    2.0.0.0
Alias           Flush-Volume                                   2.0.0.0
Alias           Get-DiskSNV                                     2.0.0.0
Alias           Get-DnsServerRRL                               2.0.0.0
Alias           Get-GPPermissions                              1.0.0.0
Alias           Get-PhysicalDiskSNV                            2.0.0.0
Alias           Get-ProvisionedAppxPackage                     3.0
Alias           Get-StorageEnclosureSNV                        2.0.0.0
Alias           Get-VpnServerIPsecConfiguration                3.0.0.0
-- More  --
```

Figure 1.3.0 - Get-Command

The information displayed in your PowerShell Console is a list of all commands that are installed on your computer. This includes cmdlets, aliases, functions, workflows, filters, scripts and applications.

There are four columns: 'CommandType', 'Name', 'Version' and 'Source'. The CommandType column shows 'Alias', 'Function' or 'Cmdlet'. The Name column shows the actual name of the cmdlet while Source column shows the name of the module that the function or Cmdlet belong to.

Note

If you are using a PowerShell edition other than 5.0, your column names will be different. All PowerShell versions other than 5.0 will have 'CommandType', 'Name' and 'ModuleName' columns. PowerShell version 5.0 has 'CommandType', 'Name' and 'Source' columns.

As you can see, executing the 'Get-Command' command without any parameters might not be very helpful. The result is too long and difficult to find any specific cmdlet.

Syntax of the Get-Command Cmdlet

The simplest syntax of the Get-Command cmdlet is:

Get-Command Command-Name

To find a specific cmdlet, enter *Get-Command* followed by the name of the cmdlet. If you know portions of the cmdlet you need, you can find the actual name of the cmdlet using wildcards.

For instance, if you wish to find all cmdlets with the Noun 'Date', execute the command below:

Get-Command *-Date

The above command will return Get-Date and Set-Date as shown in Figure 1.3.1. Notice where I placed the asterisks wildcard? I placed it that way because I know that a cmdlet Noun comes after the hyphen (-).

Figure 1.3.1 - Get-Command wildcards.

The Get-Command cmdlet is very useful when you want to find cmdlets to perform specific tasks. Recently, I was tasked with writing a PowerShell script to compare two Active Directory groups. I knew I had to find a cmdlet that contains the word 'Compare' but I did not know the full name of the cmdlet.

With my knowledge of cmdlet 'Verb-Nouns', I was able to find the cmdlet I require for my script. 'Compare' is an action word, so it has to be the verb of the cmdlet I need. So I used the Get-Command cmdlet to find the cmdlet using the command below:

Get-Command -Name compare*

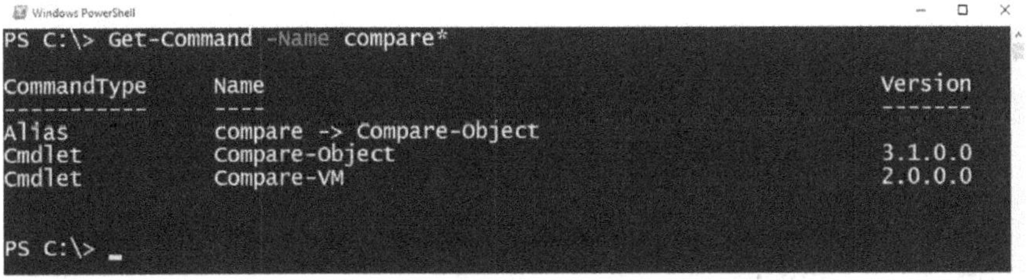

Figure 1.3.2 - Get-Command Compare

The command result has two cmdlets and one alias. From the result of the previous command, it is obvious that the cmdlet I require for my script is 'Compare-Object'. I could also use the alias for 'Compare-Object', 'Compare'.

The Get-Command cmdlet is a very useful tool to your PowerShell career. As seen in the last example, we could find a cmdlet to perform a task using the task's keyword. In this example, the task's keyword is 'compare'. You can apply this principle to most tasks in Windows.

Task 1.3.0

You want to get information about a cmdlet that you can use to backup group policy objects (GPO) , based on what you have learnt so far, what command can you run to find a cmdlet to achieve your goal?.

Section Summary

In this section we covered the following:

1. The general syntax of the Get-Command cmdlet is Get-Command Command-Name.
2. You can find cmdlet to perform specific tasks using the Get-Command cmdlet with the asterisks wildcard.

1.4 How To Use 'Verb' and 'Noun' Parameters of Get-Command

In section 1.2, we looked at cmdlet parameters. We defined a cmdlet parameter as "the mechanism that allows a cmdlet to accept input".

Among other parameters, the Get-Command cmdlet has two parameters, called 'Verb' and 'Noun'. In this tutorial, we will look at how to find cmdlets with the Get-Command cmdlet using these two parameters. Before proceed with 'Verb' and 'Noun' parameters of Get-Command, let's briefly discuss Approved PowerShell cmdlet Verbs.

Approved PowerShell Cmdlet Verbs

We already mentioned that PowerShell Cmdlets are named in Verb-Noun pairs. There are some approved verbs that are used to build cmdlets, functions and modules. Using standard verbs for cmdlet enforce consistency across cmdlets.

Approved cmdlets are grouped into 7 types: 'Common', 'Communications', 'Data', 'Diagnostic', 'Lifecycle', 'Security' and 'Other Verbs'. For a full list of the approved verbs, see reference 1, at the end of Tutorial 1. You can also get the list of approved verbs by executing the command below:

```
Get-Verb | Sort-Object Group, Verb
```

Why do you need to know the approved verbs? Two reasons. This will help you find a cmdlet you need to perform specific tasks easily. Secondly, when you start building your own functions and modules, you will need to adhere to the approved verb naming conventions.

In Tutorial 4, I will introduce Scripts, Functions and Modules. "PowerShell Tutorial Volume 3" covers Functions and Modules in details.

How to find cmdlets using Get-Command Verb and Noun Parameters

Now that you know about approved cmdlet verbs, let's see how you can apply this knowledge to find cmdlets. If you executed the previous command, you would have seen from the result that 'Get' is an approved cmdlet verb. So, if we wish to list all cmdlets that has the verb 'Get'. we would execute the command below:

Get-Command -Verb 'Get' | More

I included 'more' because the command produces a very long list. Because of the length of information, it might not be a very practical way to find cmdlets, but you get the gist. You can find cmdlets using the 'Verb' parameter of the Get-Command cmdlet. The result of the previous command is shown in Figure 1.4.0.

Figure 1.4.0 - Get-Command -Verb

You can also find cmdlets using the 'Noun' parameter. To list all cmdlets ending with the 'Noun' 'Object'. execute the command below:

Get-Command -Noun Object

The result of the command is shown in Figure 1.4.1.

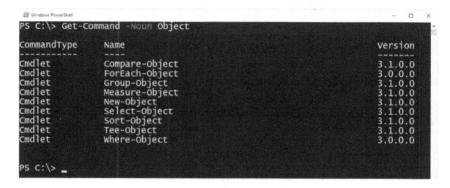

Figure 1.4.1 - Get-Command -Noun

The Get-Command cmdlet has another parameter called 'Module'. You can find all cmdlets that belong to a particular module. To execute this command, you need to know the module name or portion of the module name. To list all cmdlets that belong to the ActiveDirectory module, execute the command below:

Get-Command -Module ActiveDirectory

The result of the command is shown in Figure 1.4.2

```
Windows PowerShell                                                    —   □   ×
PS C:\> Get-Command -Module ActiveDirectory

CommandType     Name                                                    Version
-----------     ----                                                    -------
Cmdlet          Add-ADCentralAccessPolicyMember                         1.0.0.0
Cmdlet          Add-ADComputerServiceAccount                            1.0.0.0
Cmdlet          Add-ADDomainControllerPasswordReplicationPolicy         1.0.0.0
Cmdlet          Add-ADFineGrainedPasswordPolicySubject                  1.0.0.0
Cmdlet          Add-ADGroupMember                                       1.0.0.0
Cmdlet          Add-ADPrincipalGroupMembership                          1.0.0.0
Cmdlet          Add-ADResourcePropertyListMember                        1.0.0.0
Cmdlet          Clear-ADAccountExpiration                               1.0.0.0
Cmdlet          Clear-ADClaimTransformLink                              1.0.0.0
Cmdlet          Disable-ADAccount                                       1.0.0.0
Cmdlet          Disable-ADOptionalFeature                               1.0.0.0
Cmdlet          Enable-ADAccount                                        1.0.0.0
Cmdlet          Enable-ADOptionalFeature                                1.0.0.0
Cmdlet          Get-ADAccountAuthorizationGroup                         1.0.0.0
Cmdlet          Get-ADAccountResultantPasswordReplicationPolicy         1.0.0.0
Cmdlet          Get-ADAuthenticationPolicy                              1.0.0.0
Cmdlet          Get-ADAuthenticationPolicySilo                          1.0.0.0
Cmdlet          Get-ADCentralAccessPolicy                               1.0.0.0
Cmdlet          Get-ADCentralAccessRule                                 1.0.0.0
Cmdlet          Get-ADClaimTransformPolicy                              1.0.0.0
Cmdlet          Get-ADClaimType                                         1.0.0.0
```

Figure 1.4.2 - Get-Command –Module (Some results not shown in the image)

You can combine the 'Verb', 'Noun' and 'Module' parameters if you want more specific result. For example, to list all cmdlets in the ActiveDirectory module beginning with the verb 'Get' and ending with the noun containing the word 'Group', execute the command below:

Get-Command -Verb 'Get' -Noun *Group* -Module
ActiveDirectory

The command produced shorter, more specific result shown in Figure 1.4.3.

```
Windows PowerShell                                                    —   □   ×
PS C:\> Get-Command -Verb 'Get' -Noun *Group* -Module ActiveDirectory

CommandType     Name                                                    Version
-----------     ----                                                    -------
Cmdlet          Get-ADAccountAuthorizationGroup                         1.0.0.0
Cmdlet          Get-ADGroup                                             1.0.0.0
Cmdlet          Get-ADGroupMember                                       1.0.0.0
Cmdlet          Get-ADPrincipalGroupMembership                          1.0.0.0


PS C:\> _
```

Figure 1.4.3 - Get-Command -Verb -Noun -Module

Note

You can execute the Get-Command cmdlet with the 'Noun' or 'Verb' parameters alone or combined with the -Module parameter.

Section Summary

In this section we covered the following:

1. Approved cmdlets are grouped into 7 types: 'Common', 'Communications', 'Data', 'Diagnostic', 'Lifecycle', 'Security' and 'Other Verbs'.
2. You can find cmdlets using the Get-Command cmdlet with its 'Verb', 'Noun' or 'Module' parameters.

Answers to tasks in Tutorial 1

Task 1.3.0

The keyword in this task is 'Backup'. To find a cmdlet to backup GPOs, execute the command below:

Get-Command -Name Backup*

You can also execute the command

Get-Command -Name *-GPO

Both commands will produce the results shown in Figure 1.3.3

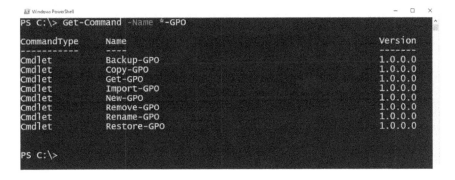

Figure 1.3.3 - Find a cmdlet to backup GPO

From Figure 1.3.3, the cmdlet we require is Backup-GPO

Downloads

Windows Management Framework 5.0 Preview April 2015 https://www.microsoft.com/en-us/download/details.aspx?id=46889

References and Further Reading

1. Approved PowerShell cmdlet Verbs https://msdn.microsoft.com/en-us/library/ms714428%28v=vs.85%29.aspx?f=255&MSPPError=-2147217396
2. Cmdlet Parameters - https://msdn.microsoft.com/en-us/library/ms714433(v=vs.85).aspx
3. Windows PowerShell https://en.wikipedia.org/wiki/Windows_PowerShell
4. Getting Started with Windows PowerShell https://technet.microsoft.com/en-us/library/hh857337.aspx
5. Reserved PowerShell Words https://technet.microsoft.com/en-us/library/Hh847868.aspx?f=255&MSPPError=-2147217396
6. Get-Command cmdlet https://technet.microsoft.com/en-us/library/hh849711.aspx

VICTOR ASHIEDU

POWERSHELL TUTORIAL 2
Getting Help With The Get-Help Cmdlet

In Tutorial 1, we discussed cmdlets and learnt how to find cmdlets using the Get-Command cmdlet. When you find a cmdlet, it is likely that you may not know how to use it. You may need things like the syntax and parameters of the cmdlet. You may also want to see examples on how to use the particular cmdlet.

Like any other tool in Windows, PowerShell has a built-in help functionality. Most PowerShell cmdlets has built-in help information. The Get-Help cmdlet provides information about any cmdlet by accessing the cmdlet's built-in help.

In addition to using the Get-Help cmdlet, you can also find help information about cmdlets online.

In Tutorial 1, we discussed PowerShell reserved words. The Get-Help cmdlet can also display help information about PowerShell reserved words. Again, there are online help information for PowerShell reserved words.

This Tutorial is dedicated to finding help about PowerShell cmdlets. Topics covered in this tutorial will be treated under the following headings:

2.0 The Get-Help command
2.1 Common parameters
2.2 Understanding a command's syntax
2.3 Detailed, Full and Online parameters
2.4 How to use the 'Examples' parameter

2.0 The Get-Help Command

In my opinion the Get-Help cmdlet is one of the most important cmdlets you will need in your PowerShell scripting career. The Get-Help cmdlet will help you find information about PowerShell commands.

The Get-Help cmdlet can display information about cmdlets, functions, CIM commands, workflows, providers, aliases and scripts. The simplest syntax of the Get-Help cmdlet is:

```
Get-Help -Name -Parameter -Full -Detailed -
Online[<CommonParameters>]
```

I have intentionally included only the parameters that you will use regularly. These parameters will be covered in this tutorial. We will discuss Common Parameters in Tutorial 2.1.

To find information about a cmdlet using the Get-Help cmdlet, simply type **Get-Help Cmdlet_Name**. Let's start by getting help about the Get-Command cmdlet. On your PowerShell console, execute the command below:

```
Get-Help -Name Get-Command
```

The result of the command is shown in Figure 2.0.0.

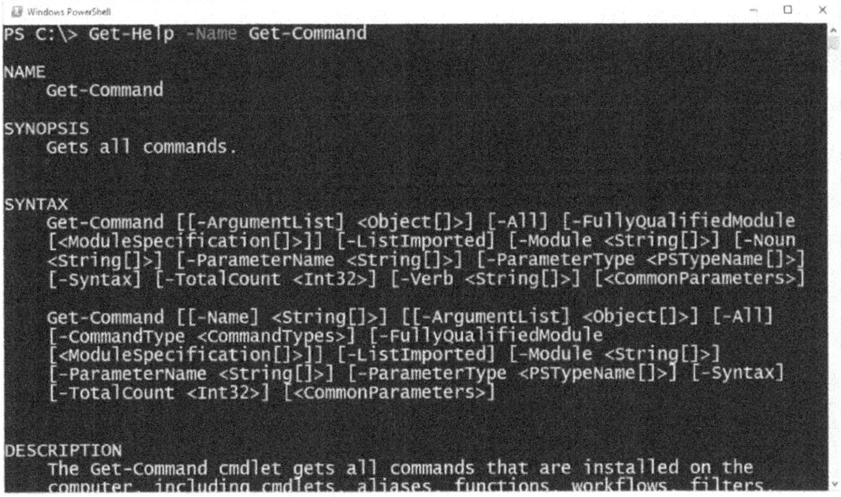

Figure 2.0.0 - Get-Help -Name Get-Command

The command displays the basic information about the Get-Command cmdlet. Information is displayed with the following sections: NAME, SYNOPSIS, SYNTAX, DESCRIPTION, RELATED LINKS and REMARKS. Take some time to read through each section.

The NAME section provides the name of the cmdlet. SYNOPSIS gives a brief summary of the cmdlet. The SYNTAX is very important. It provides how to run the command with the various parameters of the cmdlet. We will cover PowerShell syntaxes in Tutorial 2.2.

While the SYNOPSIS section provides a brief summary of the cmdlet, the DESCRIPTION section provides a detailed information about the cmdlet. If you want to get more insight into a cmdlet, read the DESCRIPTION section. I strongly recommend that you read this section when researching a cmdlet.

2.1 Common Parameters

Common parameters are a set of cmdlet parameters available for use with any cmdlet. These parameters are implemented by Windows PowerShell, and they are automatically available to any cmdlet.

In the previous tutorial, we saw that SYNTAX section is one of the sections of the result of the Get-Help command. If you look closely at the syntax of any PowerShell cmdlet, you will see <CommonParameters>. This simply means that you can use any of the in-built PowerShell Common Parameters in that cmdlet.

PowerShell Common Parameters are Verbose, Debug, ErrorAction,ErrorVariable,WarningAction,WarningVariable, OutBuffer,PipelineVariable, and OutVariable. As we progress in this book, we will cover a number of these common parameters and show you how to use them.

Let's take another look at the Get-Help Command:

Get-Help Get-Command

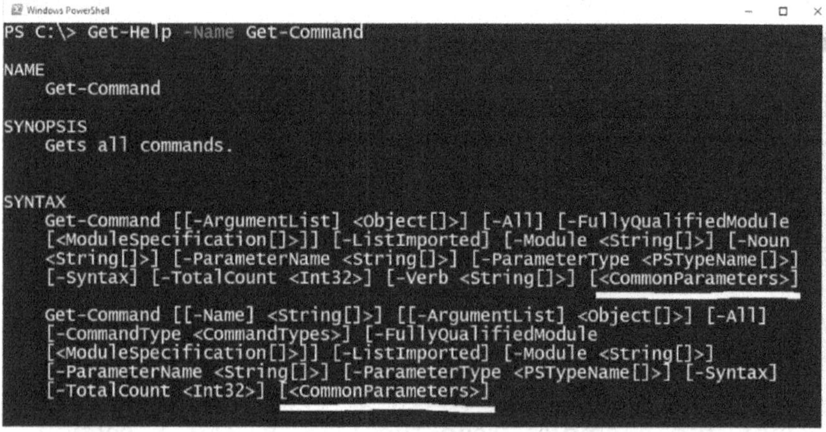

Figure 2.1.1 - Cmdlet Common Parameters (Underlined)

To illustrate the use of common parameters, let's look at the ErrorAction common parameter. If we execute the Get-Command and supply a cmdlet that does not exist, an error message is generated. For example, execute the command below:

```
Get-Command Get
```

The command returned an error as shown in Figure 2.1.2.

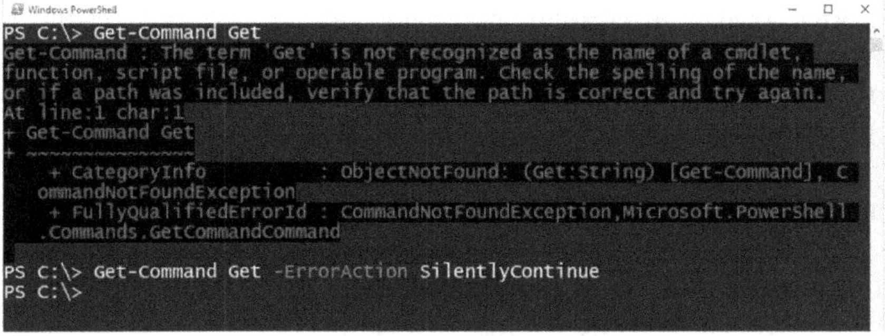

Figure 2.1.2 - Get-Command ErrorAction

When you execute the same command with the ErrorAction common parameter, the error is suppressed (Result also shown Figure 2.1.2).

```
Get-Command -Name Get -ErrorAction SilentlyContinue
```

Note

Apart from 'SilentlyContinue', the 'ErrorAction' common parameter has some other input values. To see the other available inputs, use the tab key. "PowerShell Tutorial Volume 3" covers error handling and logging.

Other Ways To Use The Get-Help Command

You can also use the Get-Help cmdlet to get information about PowerShell reserved words and other 'PowerShell Core About Topics'.

In tutorial 1.1, I introduced PowerShell reserved words. The Get-Help command can provide information about the use of these reserved words. To get information about a reserved word, for example 'IF', execute the command below:

```
Get-Help about_IF
```

The command provides a definition of the reserved word, its syntax and examples.

Notice that I appended the word 'about', to the reserved word followed by an underscore (_). Windows PowerShell also has some conceptual "About" help topics that apply to all Windows PowerShell modules. The Get-Help command provides help information about these "Core About Topics" as well.

For a full list of Windows PowerShell Core About Topics, see reference 3 at the end of this Tutorial.

Continuing with "About" topics, in tutorial 2.1, we discussed Common Parameters. There is an "About" help topic for Common Parameters. To get information about Common Parameters (including examples), execute the command below:

```
Get-Help about_CommonParameters
```

The result of the command is shown in Figure 2.1.3 below. This information can also be found online. If you 'Google' about_CommonParameters, you will get the URL for the 'about_CommonParameters' help page. For your convenience, I included this URL in reference 1 at the end of this tutorial.

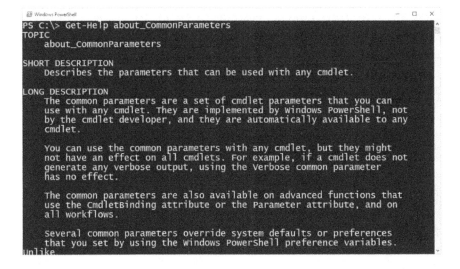

Figure 2.1.3 - Get-Help about_CommonParameters (Portions of the result not shown)

Section Summary

In this section we covered the following:

1. Common parameters are a set of cmdlet parameters available for use with any cmdlet.
2. The Common parameter, 'ErrorAction' can be used to suppress cmdlet errors.
3. The Get-Help command can get information about PowerShell reserved words and other PowerShell conceptual "About" help topics.

2.2 Understanding A Command's Syntax

A cmdlet command syntax helps you construct commands correctly. In this tutorial, I will like to dive deep into the SYNTAX section of the Get-Help command for a cmdlet. To begin execute the command:

```
Get-Help Get-ADUser -Detailed
```

Take a closer look at the SYNTAX section of the result for the above command. This section shows you how to execute the command with all the parameters listed. This is very useful as it tells you how to combine the parameters correctly. As an example, the Get-ADUser cmdlet has three syntaxes as shown in Figure 2.2.0.

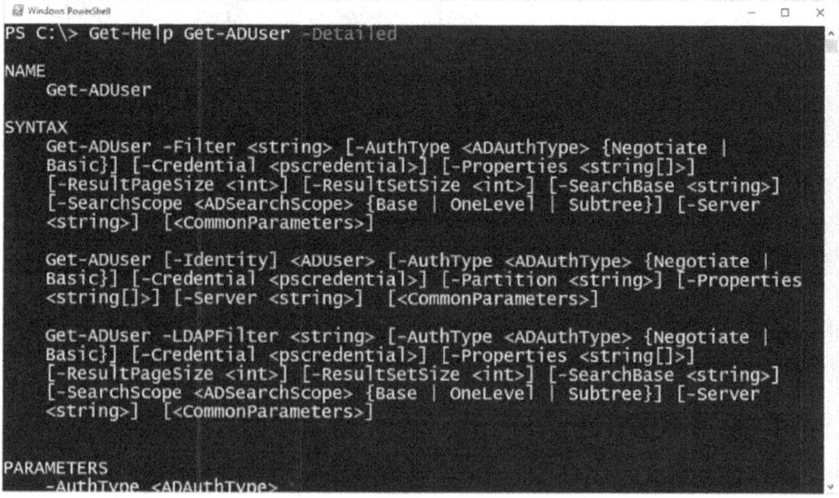

Figure 2.2.0- Get-ADUser Syntaxes

Notice that the Get-ADUser cmdlet can use the 'Filter', 'Identity' or the 'LDAPFilter' parameters. Notice also that most of the other parameters that follow these three parameters are the same with few exceptions. This is achieved by a concept called 'Parameter set name'.

Volume 3 of this book series covers 'parameter set names' in detail. The volume also discusses how to create 'parameter set names'. To find out more about parameters, see the about_parameters help topic in reference 4.

Continuing with the Get-ADUser example, we see that a cmdlet may have multiple parameters. You are only permitted to combine these parameters in particular sets. For example, you cannot use the Get-ADUser cmdlet with the 'Filter', 'Identity' and the 'LDAPFilter' parameters in the same command.

The reason you are not able to combine the three parameters in one command is because they belong to different parameter set names as seen in the SYNTAX section. If you do use any of the parameters together, it will give an error message. To illustrate this, execute the command below:

Get-ADUser -LDAPFilter "(name=Test1 User1)" -Filter {Name -eq"Test1 User1"} -Server 10.0.0.2 -Credential PSLab.local\administrator

This will generate an error as shown in Figure 2.2.1

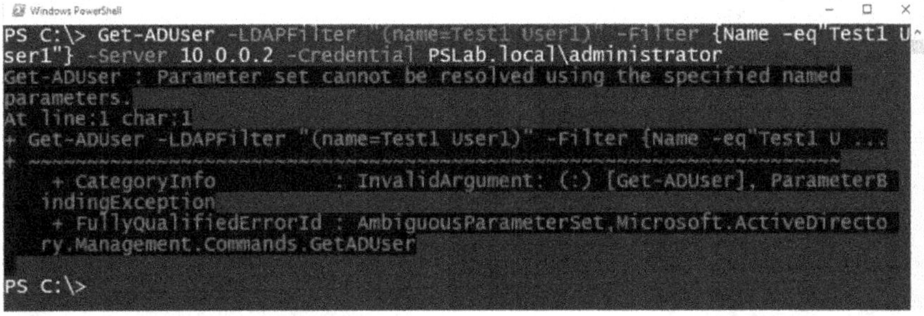

Figure 2.2.1- Get-ADUser -LDAPFilter -Filter Error

Note

Using cmdlet parameters with the wrong parameter set name combination will result in an error message **"Parameter set cannot be resolved using the specified named parameters**."

Anytime you execute a command and see this error message, it is likely that you have combined the wrong parameter set names.

The SYNTAX section of the Get-Help command will provide the correct way to combine the parameters of a cmdlet.

The correct way to combine the Get-ADUser parameters are

shown in the following commands: (Enter the password P@ssWord when prompted):

Get-ADUser -Filter {Name -eq "Test1 User1"} -Server 10.0.0.2 –Credential PSLab.local\administrator

Or

Get-ADUser -LDAPFilter "(name=test1 user1)" -Server 10.0.0.2 -Credential PSLab.local\administrator

Or

Get-ADUser -Identity Test1.User1 -Properties name -Server 10.0.0.2 -Credential PSLab.local\administrator

The commands will return the same result as shown in Figure 2.2.2

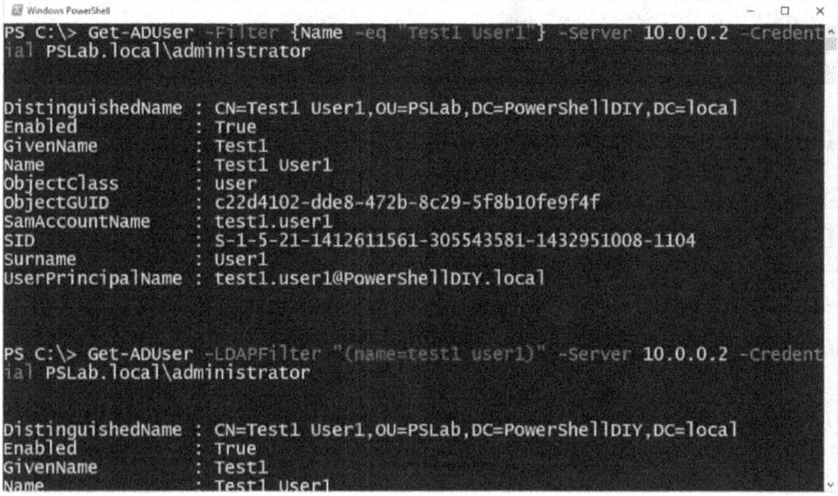

Figure 2.2.2- Get-ADUser -LDAPFilter or -Filter –Identity (Portions of the results not shown)

Info

If the Get-ADUser command returns an error, ensure that PSLabSRV server is powered on. To confirm, open PSLabSRV in Hyper-V Manager.

If the server is off, click the green power button to start it. When it is fully booted, re-run the commands. The first command might take some time to return results.

Section Summary

In this section we covered the following:

1. A cmdlet command syntax helps you construct commands correctly.
2. When you execute the Get-Help command, the SYNTAX section of the result will show you the correct way to construct commands with the cmdlet in question.
3. Using cmdlet parameters with the wrong parameter set name combination may result in an error message "Parameter set cannot be resolved using the specified named parameters."

2.3 Detailed, Full and Online Parameters

Like any other cmdlet, the Get-Help cmdlet has a number of parameters. In tutorial 2.0, we saw the basic result produced by the Get-Help Command. We can get more information using some other parameters of the Get-Help cmdlet.

To continue with the Get-Command cmdlet, to display more help information about this cmdlet, include the 'Detailed' parameter as shown below:

```
Get-Help -Name Get-Command -Detailed
```

Unlike the previous Get-Help commands, the result of the above command now includes a PARAMETERS section. The PARAMETERS section lists the parameters for the Get-Command cmdlet. See Figure 2.3.0 for details (most of the parameters are hidden in the image).

```
[Windows PowerShell                                          —  □  ×

PARAMETERS
   -All [<SwitchParameter>]
      Gets all commands, including commands of the same type that have
      the same name. By default, Get-Command gets only the commands that
      run when you type the command name.

      For more information about the method that Windows PowerShell uses
      to select the command to run when multiple commands have the same
      name, see about_Command_Precedence
      (http://go.microsoft.com/fwlink/?LinkID=113214). For information
      about module-qualified command names and running commands that do
      not run by default because of a name conflict, see about_Modules
      (http://go.microsoft.com/fwlink/?LinkID=144311).

      This parameter is introduced in Windows PowerShell 3.0.

      In Windows PowerShell 2.0, Get-Command gets all commands by default.

   -ArgumentList <Object[]>

      Gets information about a cmdlet or function when it is used with
      the specified parameters ("arguments"). The alias for
      ArgumentList is Args.
```

Figure 2.3.0 - Get-Help -Name Get-Command –Detailed

Note

Notice that in the previous command, the 'Detailed' parameter did not require any input value. This is another example of a parameter that does not require an input. Remember 'switches' parameters from Tutorial 1?

There is yet another very useful Get-Help parameter, 'Full'. The 'Full' parameter displays full help information about a cmdlet. The information provided by the 'Full' parameter, includes those provided by the 'Detailed' parameter and more. To see the effect of the 'Full' parameter, execute the command below:

Get-Help -Name Get-Command -Full

The command above will include all the sections displayed by the 'Detailed' parameter plus INPUTS, OUTPUT and EXAMPLES Sections. Compare the information listed about each parameter in Figure 2.3.0 with what is listed in Figure 2.3.1.

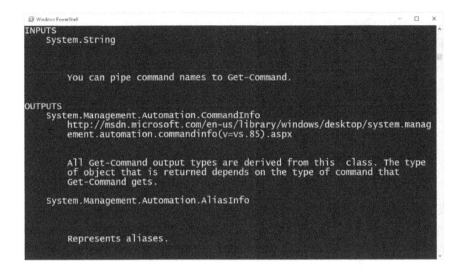

Figure 2.3.1- Get-Help Get-Command -Full

To help you understand this better, refer to Figures 2.3.0 and 2.3.1 and examine the first parameter 'All' (Some of the information is not shown in my image).

Notice that Figure 2.3.1 (please execute the command to see all results) provides additional information about whether the parameter is required or not (optional), the position of the parameter, and its default value. We also see information telling us whether the parameter accepts pipeline input (I will cover pipelines in tutorial 3.4).

The 'Full' parameter provides even more information; for example we are able to see whether the parameter accepts wildcards. These are very useful information.

The Get-Help cmdlet has two more very useful parameters: 'Example' and 'Online'. The 'Example parameter provides examples on how to use the cmdlet. The 'Online' parameter takes you to the online help page of the cmdlet. For example, to launch the help page for the Get-ChildItem cmdlet, execute the command:

```
Get-Help Get-ChildItem -Online
```

The command will launch on your default web browser. You need internet connection to display the webpage. The online version of help information is very detailed. I use this information very often when I am scripting.

Task 2.3.0

Open PowerShell console and execute the command:

```
Get-Help Get-ChildItem -Online
```

Take time to look through the information on the page. Scroll down to the end of the page and execute the commands shown in the examples.

If any of the commands continue for longer than you would wish, press Ctrl + C to stop it.

Note

The output of the Get-Help command is very similar to the online help for cmdlets. The online version normally define what the cmdlets accomplishes, gives Aliases, then Syntaxes. The online page also provides detailed description, Parameters and Examples.

Section Summary

In this section we covered the following:

1. The Get-Help cmdlet will help you find information about a cmdlet, its parameters, and examples.
2. The 'Detailed' and 'Full' parameters of the Get-Help command provides more information about a cmdlet.
3. To view the online help page of a cmdlet, use the 'Online' parameter of the Get-Help command.

2.4 How To Use The 'Examples' Parameter

The help page of PowerShell cmdlets has examples. After

reviewing all other sections, the EXAMPLES section will show you ways you can execute the cmdlet using its parameters. Sometimes, you can literally modify these examples for your scripts.

To get examples on how to use the Get-ChildItem cmdlet, execute the command below:

Get-Help Get-ChildItem -Examples

The command will show all the examples available in the Get-ChildItem help page. See Figure 2.4.0 for details.

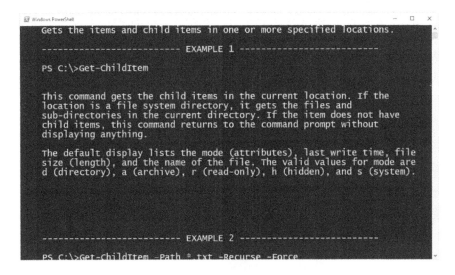

Figure 2.4.0 - Get-Help Get-ChildItem -Examples

If you performed Task 2.3.0 in tutorial 2.3, you would have noticed that the examples displayed by the previous command are similar to the examples found online for the Get-ChildItem cmdlet.

Updating Help information using Update-Help

Cmdlet help information stored on your computer may

become obsolete. If you ever need to update this information, there is a cmdlet that does this, Update-Help! Sound like a cmdlet? Yes, 'Update' is the cmdlet Verb, 'Help' is the Noun.

As you would expect, the Update-Help cmdlet has a number of parameters, but we would stick with the basic command. To update the help information for cmdlets in your computer, execute the command below:

```
Update-Help
```

The above command will take some time to complete; as it downloads the newest help files for Windows PowerShell modules and installs them on your computer. While the command is executing, it will display information similar to Figure 2.4.1.

Figure 2.4.1 - Update-Help

Note

The Update-Help command may return some errors. The error may be related to *"Update-Help : Failed to update Help for the module(s)"*. This is most likely because the command was not able to find help files for some modules online.

If you want to get more information about the Update-Help cmdlet, execute the command below:

Get-Help Update-Help -Detailed

Section Summary

In this section we covered the following:

1. The EXAMPLES section of a Get-Help command result will show you ways you can execute the cmdlet using its parameters.
2. You can access a cmdlet's usage examples by executing the Get-Help command with the 'Examples' parameter. You can also access this information on the online page of the cmdlet.
3. The Update-Help cmdlet updates the help information of PowerShell modules on your computer to the newest version.

References and Further Reading

1. about_CommonParameters
   https://technet.microsoft.com/en-us/library/hh847884.aspx?f=255&MSPPError=-2147217396
2. about_Command_Syntax
   https://technet.microsoft.com/en-us/library/hh847867.aspx
3. PowerShell Core About Topics
   https://technet.microsoft.com/en-us/library/hh847856.aspx
4. about_Parameters
   https://technet.microsoft.com/en-us/library/hh847824.aspx

VICTOR ASHIEDU

POWERSHELL TUTORIAL 3
Variables And Pipelines

A PowerShell variable stores information from commands or information to be used as inputs to commands. In this tutorial, you will learn the different types of variables. You will also learn how to create, access and manipulate variables.

This tutorial will also teach you PowerShell pipelines. A pipeline allows you to use the output of one command as the input of the next command.

Topics covered in this Tutorial will be treated under the following headings:

3.0 What are PowerShell variables?
3.1 Automatic variables
3.2 Environment variables
3.3 Variables and quoting rules
3.4 PowerShell pipelines

3.0 What Are PowerShell Variables?

As defined in the about_variables help page, "A variable is a unit of memory in which values are stored". This sounds good but it doesn't do you much good, does it?

It simply means that a variable stores results of commands in it. It could also store elements that are used in commands and expressions. Let's just cut the talk and take some examples.

A variable is represented by text strings (letters) that begin with a dollar sign ($). An example of a variable is $VarTest.

In this example, the text string is 'VarTest'. It begins with a dollar sign ($). It is that straight forward!

Note

In Windows PowerShell, variables are represented by text strings that begin with a dollar sign ($).

Open your PowerShell console and execute the command below:

$VarTest = Get-Process | Where-Object {$_.ProcessName - eq 'svchost'}

Notice that the command did not return any output to the console.

Now, execute the command on the right hand side of the equal (=) sign as shown below:

Get-Process | Where-Object {$_.ProcessName -eq 'svchost'}

Woola! We have some information as shown in Figure 3.0.1

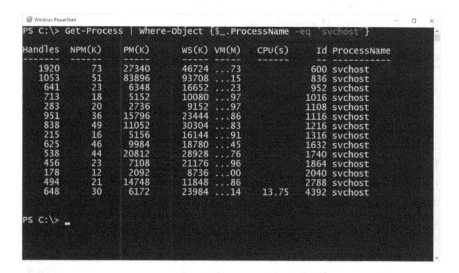

Figure 3.0.1 - Variable and Pipe example 1

I guess the next valid question would be "What happened to the information in the first command?" The answer is very simple. It was stored in the $VarTest variable. To confirm this, execute the Clear-Host command to clear your PowerShell console, then execute the command below:

```
$VarTest
```

We have exactly the same result! See Figure 3.0.2 below. Compare Figure 3.0.2 with Figure 3.0.1.

```
Windows PowerShell                                                    —    □    ×
PS C:\> $VarTest

Handles  NPM(K)    PM(K)     WS(K) VM(M)   CPU(s)      Id ProcessName
-------  ------    -----     ----- -----   ------      -- -----------
   1915      73    27272     46688 ...72              600 svchost
   1053      51    83656     93468 ...15              836 svchost
    640      23     6348     16648 ...23              952 svchost
    717      18     5200     10132 ...97             1016 svchost
    283      20     2736      9152 ...97             1108 svchost
    951      36    15800     23452 ...86             1116 svchost
    838      49    11040     30300 ...83             1216 svchost
    215      16     5156     16144 ...91             1316 svchost
    625      46     9940     18748 ...45             1632 svchost
    538      44    20828     28944 ...76             1740 svchost
    456      23     7100     21168 ...96             1864 svchost
    178      12     2092      8736 ...00             2040 svchost
    494      21    14748     11848 ...86             2788 svchost
    648      30     6172     23984 ...14    13.75    4392 svchost

PS C:\> _
```

Figure 3.0.2 – Command stored in $VarTest variable

Variables are very useful when developing complex PowerShell scripts and functions. One use of variables is to reduce typing repetitive information in different parts of your script.

When you define a variable, you are able to use the same variable in different parts of your script where the same information is required. You will discover other applications of variables as we progress.

Other Ways To Create And Manipulate Variables.

One way to create variables is to name the variable and assign a value to it as shown in the previous example. There are also a number of cmdlets that contain the 'Noun' 'Variable'. These cmdlets are used to create, edit and remove variables. To get a list of these cmdlets, execute the command below:

```
Get-Command -Noun Variable
```

Task 3.0.0

See whether you can figure out what each of the cmdlets listed by the previous command. What command can help you find this information?

Let's start with Get-Variable cmdlet. Execute the command below:

```
Get-Variable
```

The command lists all variables in the current console. This includes variables you created and variables created and maintained by Windows PowerShell. If you scroll down, you will see the variable we created earlier, 'VarTest' in the list.

When we created 'VarTest' variable, it had values assigned to it. These values were assigned by the command after the equal (=) sign. Let's confirm that these values are still stored in this variable. Execute the command below:

```
$VarTest
```

Let's clear the values in the variables using the Clear-Variable command.

```
Clear-Variable VarTest
```

Note

When executing any of the 'Variable' cmdlets, do not append the dollar sign to the variable. For example, if you executed the previous command with the dollar sign, it will return an error.

Now that you have cleared the values stored in VarTest variable, if you execute the command below, it will not return any value. To confirm this, execute the command below:

```
$VarTest
```

We could delete 'VarTest' variable completely by executing the command below:

```
Remove-Variable VarTest
```

Note

Variable names are not case-sensitive. They can include spaces and special characters, but it is recommended to avoid spaces and special characters as these are difficult to use.

Types of Variables

There are different types of variables in Windows PowerShell. This tutorial will cover the following:

User-created variables

A User-created variable is a variable created by a user. By default, when you create a variable, it only exists on the current PowerShell console it was created. An example of a User-created variable is 'VarTest' created in the previous tutorial.

Automatic variables

Automatic variables are created by Windows PowerShell to store its states. All changes to an automatic variable is done by Windows PowerShell. You cannot change an automatic variable but you can work with them. An example of an automatic variable is '$_' or '$PSItem'.

To find out about automatic variables including examples, execute the command below:

Get-Help about_automatic_variables

Environment variables

While automatic variables store information about the PowerShell environment, environment variables store information about the operating system environment.

Information such as the operating system path, WINDIR and the number of processors, are stored in environment variables. Unlike automatic variables, environment variables can be changed by a user.

3.1 Automatic Variables

As mentioned earlier, an example of automatic variable that you will meet very often as you script in PowerShell is '$_'. Dollar sign, followed by an underscore.

There are a number of automatic variables but I will only cover the once you will likely use often - $Error, $True, $False, $Null and $MyInvocation. I will provide detailed examples of the usage and applications of these automatic variables but I will like to give a quick summary of their definitions. See Table 3.0.0 for details.

S/N	Automatic Variables	Definition
1	$_	Contains the current object in the pipeline object
2	$Error	Contains an array of error

		objects that represent the most recent errors
3	$True	Contains the value 'TRUE'.
4	$False	Contains the value 'FALSE'
5	$Null	Contains a NULL or empty value
6	$MyInvocation	Contains an information about the current command

Table 3.0.0 - Common Automatic Variables

To read more about Environment Variables and Preference Variables, see reference numbers 5 and 6 respectively (End of this tutorial).

The $_ Automatic Variable

When you execute the command *Get-Process*, the column headers shown in Figure 3.1.0 will be stored in an automatic variable $_

```
Windows PowerShell                                               -  □  ×
PS C:\> Get-Process

Handles  NPM(K)    PM(K)      WS(K) VM(M)    CPU(s)     Id ProcessName
-------  ------    -----      ----- -----    ------     -- -----------
    446      36    28356      29356   297 ...51.03    1620 AcroRd32
    348      18     8136      10884   108    3.83     8652 AcroRd32
    253      15     2932       1604    98    1.69     8716 AdobeARM
     48       4      624       2836    14             1872 AERTSr64
    279      31     5952      14036   140             1900 AppleMobileDevi...
    295      22    19012      28872 ...31    2.42     3428 ApplicationFram...
    110       8     1240       5280    53             1856 armsvc
    177      11     9612      12052 ...14    0.27     8512 audiodg
    276      29    65880      37252   331   35.88     4460 chrome
    218      23    44872      31912   221   66.36     6096 chrome
   1869     101    96428      83684   505  230.23     6704 chrome
    248      29    75712      44804   292   39.89     7712 chrome
    271      37   125260      97204   355   97.98     7736 chrome
    286      27    95900      14920   312   33.69     8988 chrome
    229      26    42448      25368   216    7.84     9028 chrome
    269      37   126244     107092   368  108.14     9612 chrome
    235      25    53368      25984   242    3.97     9732 chrome
     39       4     2592       2668 ...66    0.06     7444 cmd
     87       7     1384       4996 ...29    0.05     1524 conhost
    131      11     4704      10896 ...40   11.03     4172 conhost
    140      12     4184      12928    57    8.52     6456 conhost
```

Figure 3.1.0 - Automatic Variable '$_'

Each column is represented by the automatic variable $_, followed by a dot (.) then the column name. For example

$_.Handles, $_.NPM and $_.ProcessName. To confirm this, open a PowerShell console and execute the command below:

```
Get-Process | Where-Object {$_.
```

Press the tab key to scroll through the properties (shown as column names in Figure 3.1.0). You will notice some properties are not shown in Figure 3.1.0. The reason for this is that by default, not all properties are display by the Get-Process command.

The example below further illustrates, the use of automatic variable, $_. Open a new editor (File => New) in PowerGUI Script Editor. On the new editor. Enter the following lines:

```
Get-Content '<DriveName>:\PSLab\Tutorial
3\ServerFile.txt' | ForEach-Object {

Write-Host "Server name is $_"

}
```

Highlight the whole text, right-click and select 'Execute Selection'. This will display the output shown in Figure 3.1.1. From the result of the command, you can deduce that the variable $_, stored the names of each server found in the text file and returned by the *Get-Content* command.

You have written your first PowerShell script! To save the script, from File menu of PowerGUI, select "Save As", navigate to "<DriveName>:\PSLab\MyScripts\Tutorial 3" and enter EchoServerNames as the name of the script. Beside "Save as type" note the file extension, "PowerShell Scripts (*.ps1) and click Save.

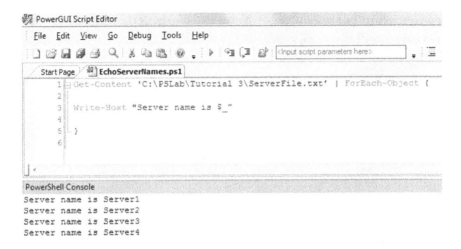

Figure 3.1.1 - Automatic Variable Example 1

The $Error Automatic Variable

Another automatic variable is $Error. To examine the power of $Error automatic variable, execute the command below in your PowerShell console:

```
$Error
```

The command above will likely display a long list of errors that have been logged on your PowerShell console. If the $Error variable does not return any errors, it means that no error(s) have been stored in the variable.

The $Error automatic variable contains an array of error objects that represent the most recent errors. To clear all the errors stored in the $Error variable and clear your PowerShell console, execute the commands below, one at a time:

```
$Error.clear()
Clear-Host
```

The $Error.clear() command clears all errors stored in the $Error automatic variable, while the Clear-Host command clears your console. Now, if you execute $Error command, no error will be displayed.

Let's now execute some commands that will store some errors in the $Error automatic variable. Execute the following commands for a non-existing computer, 'TestComputer':

Get-Process -ComputerName TestComputer

The command will take some time to execute before returning an error message "Get-Process: Couldn't connect to remote machine." Execute a second command to generate another error:

Get-WmiObject -Class Win32_OperatingSystem - ComputerName TestComputer

This generates an error message "Get-WmiObject: The RPC server is unavailable. (Exception from HRESULT: 0x800706BA)". You should now have two error messages as shown in Figure 3.1.2.

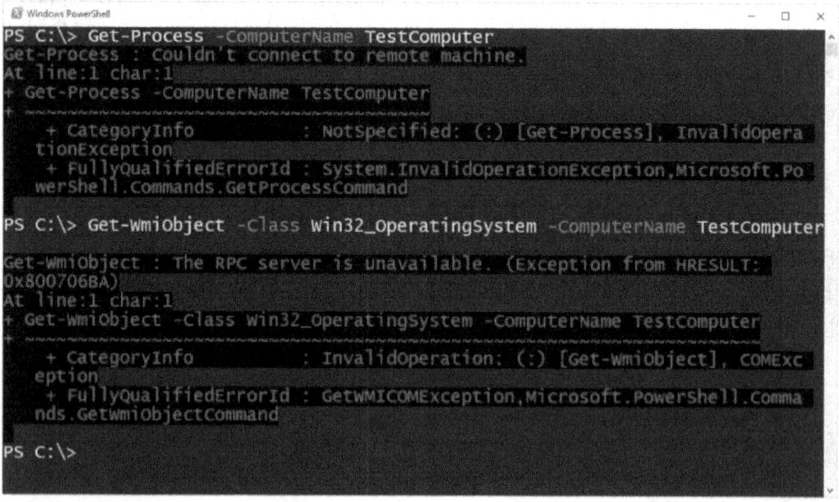

Figure 3.1.2 - $Error Messages

Clear your PowerShell console using the Clear-Host command and execute $Error to display the most recent errors. The two errors shown in Figure 3.1.2 should be displayed. To display the last error, execute $Error[0]. To display the first error, execute $Error[1]. This information can be very useful when scripting; if you wish to capture and display errors.

The $Error automatic variable has a number of other properties and methods that can be very useful. For instance, we can count the number of errors stored in the variable by executing $Error.Count. A very good way to use this information in a script may be to execute the $Error.clear() command at the beginning of your script to clear all errors.

Then, to inform the user the number of errors generated, you could then execute the script below:

```
Write-Host ""$Error.Count" errors were generated during
the execution of this script"
```

The command above will display the message "*2 errors were generated during the execution of this script*" without the quotes. If you have more than two errors stored in your $Error automatic variable, you might have a different message.

I will discuss object properties and how to find and use them in Tutorial 7. Volume 3 of this book series covers errors, including handling and logging. For your personal practice, open a new PowerGUI editor and enter the following lines:

```
$Error.clear()
Get-Process -ComputerNameTestComputer
Get-WmiObject -Class Win32_OperatingSystem -
ComputerName TestComputer
Write-Host ""$Error.Count" errors were generated during
the execution of this script"
```

Right-click the whole text and select 'Execute Selection'. What we have done is to put all the commands we executed above in a script.

Note

A script is a plain text file that contains one or more Windows PowerShell commands. We have used PowerGUI, not a text file to create the script above.

In our script, line 1 clears all errors stored in the $Error automatic variable. The two commands that follow, execute and return errors as shown earlier; while the last command counts the number of errors stored in the $Error variable and displays a message on the console. Save this script in "<DriveName>:\PSLab\MyScripts\Tutorial 3" as ClearCountErrors.ps1.

$True, $False and $Null Automatic Variables

These variables can help you check if an expression or command is true, false or null (empty value). To continue with the $Error variable example, let's execute a command that displays a message if the $Error automatic variable is $Null.

Open a new PowerGUI editor and enter the following:

```
If (!$Error)

{Write-Host "No error message was generated"}

ElseIf ($Error)

{Write-Host ""$Error.Count" errors were generated during
the execution of this script"}
```

The command checks the $Error automatic variable. If there is no information found in the variable, it displays the message *"No error message was generated"*. Else If the variable contains information, it displays the error count information: *"2 errors were generated during the execution of this script"*. You can apply this concept in various ways in a script.

Save the script as <DriveName>:\PSLab\MyScripts\Tutorial 3\$ErrorVariable.ps1

Task 3.1.0

Referring to the previous script, if you want to ensure that the message: "No error message was generated" is displayed, what command will you add on top of this script?

To further illustrate the use of $True and $False variables. Execute the following commands (One line at a time):

```
Test-Connection www.google.com -BufferSize 16 -Quiet -
Count 2
Test-Connection google -BufferSize 16 -Quiet -Count 2
```

The commands will return 'True' and 'False' respectively. The Test-Connection cmdlet with the -Quiet parameter pings a host and returns a value of 'True' if the host replies successfully and 'False' if the ping fails.

I have used this in so many scripts that involves performing a task on multiple hosts. This is necessary because it helps confirm that a host is online before attempting to perform a remote task on the host.

Scenario Application

You receive a request from your line manager to find the IP addresses of 5 websites. Your line manager sends the names of the websites in a text file called WebsiteNames.txt.

This file is located in <DrivePath>:\PSLab\Tutorial 3. You are required to return the IP address of the website if you are able to ping it.

We will build the script step by step. To complete the task, open a blank PowerGUI editor and add the lines shown in the boxes below:

Step 1: Create a variable that will store the website names. Call the variable $WebsiteNames.

```
$WebsiteNames = Get-Content
'<DriveName>:\PSLab\Tutorial 3\WebsiteNames.txt'
```

Step 2: Pipe the output of the $WebsiteNames variable to a ForEach-Object loop as shown below (Add the lines below beneath the previous line):

```
$WebsiteNames | ForEach-Object {


}
```

Step 3: The next step is to perform the actual ping using the Test-Connection cmdlet as shown in our previous command. These commands will be placed within the ForEach-Object statement block.

Remember our automatic variable '$_'? We will use it here again. We will simply replace the name of the website in the command below with the automatic variable, $_. Modify your script as shown below:

```
$WebsiteNames | ForEach-Object {

Test-Connection $_ -BufferSize 16 -Quiet -Count 2

}
```

This is how you build a script; one line at a time. If we combine the scripts, we will have the following:

```
$WebsiteNames = Get-Content '<DriveName>:\PSLab\
Tutorial 3\WebsiteNames.txt'

$WebsiteNames | ForEach-Object {

Test-Connection $_ -BufferSize 16 -Quiet -Count 2

}
```

After typing in the texts above into your PowerGUI editor, highlight the whole text, right-click and select 'Execute Selection'. Beneath the console, the result will display 'True', 'False', 'True', 'True', 'False'. If you review the content of the text file, you will understand the result.

To put it in context, try pinging each of the sites shown in the text file. The ones that reply are the ones that displayed 'True', while the ones that 'times out' showed 'False' to the Test-Connection command above.

We have more tasks to accomplish with our script. The final task is to return the IP address of the website if and only if the website returns a reply (True). This is where we will apply our $True or $False automatic variable. This information lies within the output of the Test-Connection command.

Step 4: To return the IP address of the websites, we would have to loop through the output of the Test-Connection command. This will be accomplished by piping (|) it to yet another ForEach-Object. So our script will now look like this:

```
$WebsiteNames = Get-Content 'E:\PSLab\Tutorial
3\WebsiteNames.txt'

$WebsiteNames | ForEach-Object {

    Test-Connection $_ -BufferSize 16 -Quiet -Count 2 |
    ForEach-Object {

    }

}
```

Step 5: The next step will be to test the output of the Test-Connection command for $True or $False. We will only return IP address of the websites that respond to ping. To accomplish this, we will use an 'If'
statement. The script will look like this:

```
$WebsiteNames = Get-Content 'E:\PSLab\Tutorial
3\WebsiteNames.txt'

$WebsiteNames | ForEach-Object {

    Test-Connection $_ -BufferSize 16 -Quiet -Count 2 |
    ForEach-Object {

    If ($_ -eq '$True') {

    #Add further commands here

}
    }
```

```
}
```

Displaying the IP address of the websites will require an understanding of object properties. I will introduce you to object properties in Tutorial 7. We will complete this portion of the task in section 2.1. Before we proceed, let's save our script. Save it as WebsiteNames in this location: <DriveLetter>:\PSLab\MyScripts\Tutorial 3\WebsiteNames.ps1

Note

In our last script, we used the $_ automatic variable twice. It is important to understand that they represent different objects at each ForEach-Object loop.

In the first loop, $_ represented the names of the websites; at the second ForEach-Object loop, $_ automatic variable represented 'True' or 'False', the output of the Test-Connection command.

Section Summary

In this section we covered the following:

1. An example of automatic variable is '$_'. Dollar sign, followed by an underscore.
2. Other automatic variables are $Error, $True, $False, $Null and $MyInvocation.
3. To access the properties of a command using the '$_' automatic variable, enter $_, followed by a dot (.) then the name of the property you wish to access.
4. The $Error automatic variable contains an array of error objects that represent the most recent errors.
5. The $True, $False and $Null Automatic Variables can help you check if an expression or command is true, false or null (empty value).

3.2 Environment Variables

Open a PowerShell console and execute the command below:

Get-ChildItem env:

The command lists environment variables on your computer. Figure 3.2.0 shows my result. Is this different from yours?

Figure 3.2.0 - Get-ChildItem env

Like automatic variables, these are inbuilt; you do not assign them. Let's discover these variables by utilizing the command completion functionality of PowerShell. Open a new PowerShell console and type the lines below:

$Env:

Now, press the Tab key to display the first variable. Keep pressing the Tab key until the console displays COMPUTERNAME as shown below:

$Env: COMPUTERNAME

Hit your Enter key to execute the command. The result? The name of your computer! Delete COMPUTERNAME, enter the letter H and restart Tab key again until you reach HOMEPATH. Again, hit enter key to execute the command. The result is \Users\<UserName>.

Let me introduce another way of finding environment variables, '[Environment]:' To discover the power of this variable, enter [Environment] followed by two colons (::) in your PowerGUI editor. Your command should look like:

[Environment]::

Once you enter the colons beside [Environment], PowerGUI displays a whole set of available options as shown in Figure 3.2.1.

Figure 3.2.1 - [Environment] Variables

Again, you can explore these values one by one to see the results. Scroll down and select MachineName as shown below:

```
[Environment]::MachineName
```

The result should be obvious. Execute the command to confirm your suspicion. It is your computer name indeed!

Refer to Figure 3.2.1. Notice that PowerGUI displays two sets of objects. Some of them are 'Properties'; for example MachineName as seen in our previous example. Others are called 'Methods'. Methods allow you to execute further commands. An example of a Method is GetFolderPath. To locate this method, type [Environment]:: in a PowerGUI editor, scroll to GetFolderPath and select it.

If you execute this command, it will return *OverloadDefinitions* error. This is not useful. To make use of this method, you have to include bracket open and close () after GetFolderPath. Your command should look like the one below:

```
[Environment]::GetFolderPath()
```

Again, executing this command returns an error. The reason being that the method is expecting an input. Okay, let's tell the command to find the path to your "My Documents" folder. Now include "MyDocuments", including the double quotes in the bracket as shown below:

```
[Environment]::GetFolderPath("MyDocuments")
```

Now we have a very useful result: full path to your "Documents" folder! I will dig deeper into Object Properties and Methods in Tutorial 7.

Some Applications Of Environment Variables

I have shown you some environment variables, but how do you utilize this powerful functionality in PowerShell scripting? I have used these variables in some of my scripts and I will illustrate with one of them.

Recently, I built a function that reports a computer's last boot time. I called it Get-ComputerBootTime. You can download the function from download reference 2 at the end of this tutorial. The function gets the last boot time of a local or remote computer(s). When I execute Get-ComputerBootTime on my laptop, the result is shown in figure 3.2.2.

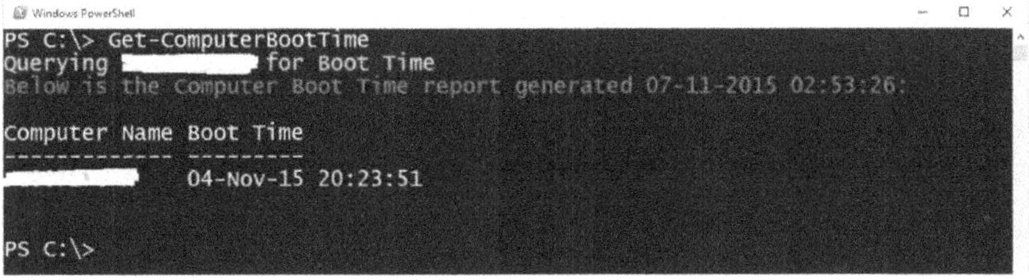

Figure 3.2.2 - Get-ComputerBootTime function

The Get-ComputerBootTime function has two parameters that can accept a computer's name: ComputerName or ComputerNameFile.

When you specify the ComputerName parameter, you can enter a computer name or multiple computer names to report last boot time. If you specify the ComputerNameFile parameter, you enter the location of a text file containing a list of computer names to query for last boot time.

To build the script that executes the function, I needed to combine the ComputerName and ComputerNameFile parameters into a single variable. The thought behind this is so that no matter the parameter the user calls, I will feed only one variable into my script.

To build the script, I proceeded with the steps outlined below:

Step 1: Define a variable called $ComputerNames

Step 2: Next, I used the 'If' Statement to determine the content of the $ComputerNames variable depending on the parameter used. Below is the first part of the script:

```
$ComputerNames =

If ($ComputerNameFile)

{ Get-Content $ComputerNameFile }
```

If you recollect, the ComputerNameFile parameter takes input from a text file; therefore, we needed to retrieve the computer names from the text file using the Get-Content cmdlet.

The previous command block determines whether the ComputerNameFile parameter has been called – represented by 'If ($ComputerNameFile)'. If it is called, the script executes the Get-Content command to retrieve the contents of the specified text file.

Step 3: The next step is to determine how the script behaves when the ComputerName parameter is called. I extended the script as shown below:

```
$ComputerNames =

If ($ComputerNameFile)

{ Get-Content $ComputerNameFile }

ElseIf ($ComputerName)

{$ComputerName}
```

Info

Volume 2 of the "PowerShell Tutorial" book series covers 'IF' statements in detail. Just to bring you up to speed, the 'IF' statements syntax is shown below:

```
If (Condition1) {Perform action 1}
ElseIf (Condition2) {Perform action 2}
Else {Perform action 3 }.
```

In the ongoing command examples, I have put the 'If' statements in capitals for easy identification. $ComputerNames is the common variable that I will feed into the script that executes the Get-ComputerBootTime function.

Step 4: The last stage that demonstrates how I combined the parameters used in the Get-ComputerBootTime function is where I applied the $env:COMPUTERNAME environment variable.

Note that in the command, I have already used 'If' and then 'ElseIf'. If I add the last stage of the 'If' statement block, I will achieve my intentions. The final script looks like this:

```
$ComputerNames =

If ($ComputerNameFile)
{ Get-Content $ComputerNameFile }

ElseIf ($ComputerName)
{$ComputerName}

Else
{$env:COMPUTERNAME }
```

What does this achieve? If the ComputerNameFile parameter is called, get the contents of the text file specified. Else, if the ComputerName parameter is called, list the

VICTOR ASHIEDU

names of the computers as listed in the console.

Finally, if none of these two parameters are specified, the script assumes that the user wants to query the local computer for last boot time and fetch this information using the '$env:COMPUTERNAME' environmental variable.

This was exactly what happened when I executed the command shown in Figure 3.2.2. The function queried my local computer since I did not provide any input.

This is just one example of what you can achieve with built-in environmental variables. As you progress, you will meet other examples. Please open a new PowerGUI editor and type out the last command as shown. Save the script as Get-ComputerBootTime.psm1.

On the new editor in PowerGUI, click 'File', select 'Save As'; and on the file name, enter Get-ComputerBootTime then on the 'Save as type', select 'PowerShell Module Files'. Save the file to '<DriveName>:\PSLab\MyScripts\Tutorial 3.

$Script:MyInvocation.MyCommand.Path

Sometimes, you might need to access the location where your current script is executing from. For example, you might want to drop reports in that location, or create an error log text file.

There are just so many reasons why you might want to automatically determine the location (folder path) where your script is located or executing from. This can be achieved using the $script:MyInvocation.MyCommand.Path automatic variable. Before we proceed, open a new PowerGUI editor and enter the following lines:

```
Split-Path $script:MyInvocation.MyCommand.Path
```

The command above should display the location of your current script but it does not.

Highlight the whole line above in PowerGUI, right-click it and select 'Execute Selection'. Executing the command will throw the error message *"Split-Path: Cannot bind argument to parameter 'Path' because it is null."* Split-Path will normally return the script path based on the command above.

Why did it return the error message? The reason is simple, the $script:MyInvocation.MyCommand.Path automatic variable only populates when you are executing a script off the PowerShell console.

To demonstrate this, save the file as "<DriveName>:\PSLab\MyScripts\Tutorial 3\MyCommandPath.ps1'. Open PowerShell console, and change directory to the location of the script as shown below (Change drive letter accordingly):

```
Set-Location' <DriveName>:\PSLab\MyScripts\Tutorial 3'
```

Note

The alias for Set-Location is cd or Change Directory. This is similar to the cd (change directory) command used in Command Prompt.

On the PowerShell console, enter a dot (.) followed by a backslash (\). Use the command completion functionality to find the scripts in that location (by pressing the Tab key). Press the Tab key until you locate MyCommandPath.ps1 as shown in Figure 3.2.4, then execute it by pressing the Enter key.

The console will display the location of the script – highlighted in Figure 3.2.3.

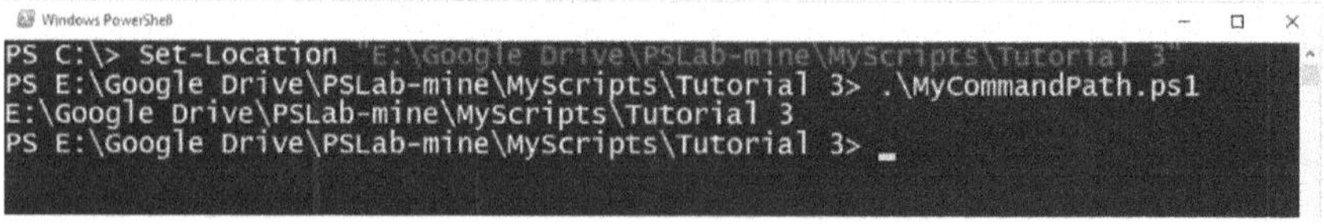

Figure 3.2.3 - MyCommandPath

Section Summary

In this section we covered the following:

1. The command "Get-ChildItem env:" will list the environment variables on your computer.
2. You can also access environment variables using "$Env:" and "[Environment]::".
3. One application of environment variable in scripting is to determine the local computer name using the command "$env:COMPUTERNAME" or "[Environment]::MachineName"
4. You can determine the path your script is executing from using the "$script:MyInvocation.MyCommand.Path automatic variable" environment variable.
5. The "$script:MyInvocation.MyCommand.Path" will only provide a result if executed off a PowerShell console.

3.3 Variables And Quoting Rules

In Windows PowerShell, quotation marks are used to specify a literal string. You can enclose a string in single quotation marks (') or double quotation marks ("). A regular string literal consists of zero or more characters enclosed in double quotes.

Single (') or Double ("") and Variables

When defining variables, you can use single (') or Double ("") quotes. The quote mark you use will determine how PowerShell processes the variable. Execute (type then press the Enter key) the following commands in a PowerShell console, one line at a time:

```
$QuoteTest = 5
$SingleQuote = '$QuoteTest'
$DoubleQuote = "$QuoteTest"
```

To see the result of single (") or Double (""), execute each of the variables below, one line at a time:

```
$SingleQuote
$DoubleQuote
```

The output is shown in Figure 3.3.0.

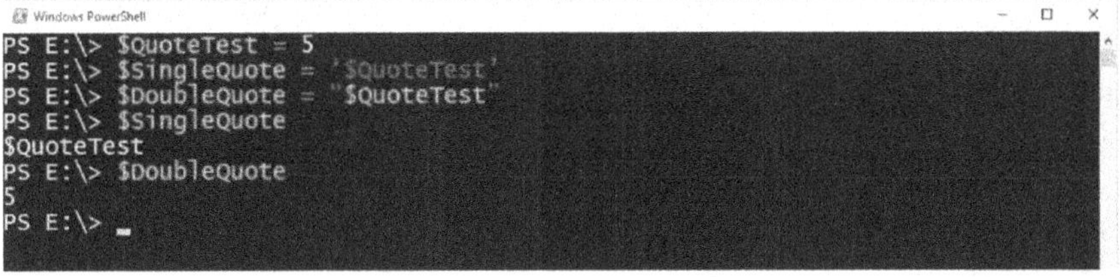

Figure 3.3.0 - Single-Double-Quote-Examples

Notice that the variable $QuoteTest, which is equals 5 is displayed when enclosed in a Double ("") quote but it is displayed as $QuoteTest when enclosed in a single (") quote.

Practical Application of Quoting Rules

Recently I was faced with a dilemma when I was building a script that Uninstalled patches from Windows Server 2003 Servers - don't ask me why I still have Windows Server 2003 in my environment!

To build the script, I used the Invoke-WmiMethod cmdlet to call the spuninst.exe utility. This is the utility that uninstalls a specific patch from Windows Server 2003. The spuninst.exe utility is located in the path 'C:\WINDOWS\$NtUninstallKB3002657$\spuninst\'. Where KB3002657 is the patch ID.

Notice that 'NtUninstallKB3002657' is enclosed in Dollar ($)

signs. This is the same sign that PowerShell uses to identify variables. As expected, this could cause some troubles.

To proceed with my script, I needed to check whether the spuninst.exe utility exists before I attempted to uninstall the patch. One way to achieve this was to Test the path '\\$Computer\c$\WINDOWS\$NtUninstallKB3002657$\s puninst\spuninst.exe'. When I tested the script, I realized that Test-Path returned error 'file does not exist' even when the file existed.

What was the problem? It took sometime before I realized what the problem was - the existence of \$NtUninstallKB3002657$\ in the path. PowerShell was interpreting $NtUninstallKB3002657$ as a variable rather than a string.

To resolve this problem, I needed to find a way to tell PowerShell that $NtUninstallKB3002657$ should be displayed exactly as it is (a string) and not interpreted as a variable. One way to achieve this is to store $NtUninstallKB3002657$ in a variable using the single (") quote rule. So I stored $NtUninstallKB3002657$ in a variable called $Uniquepath as shown below:

```
$Uniquepath = '$NtUninstallKB3002657$'
```

Then I replaced $NtUninstallKB3002657$ with the variable, $Uniquepath as illustrated below:

```
$Computer = "TestComputer"
$spuninstpath =
"\\$Computer\c$\WINDOWS\$Uniquepath\spuninst\spun
inst.exe"
```

Note

I used the UNC path '\\$Computer\c$\WINDOWS' because my script connects to the computer remotely. In the previous command, it is necessary to define the $Computer variable because it is required by the second command. For the purposes of this practice script, if this was omitted, the final result will be incomplete.

This approach resolved my challenge and my script executed successfully. To drive the point home, let's play around with the commands. Execute the commands in order (execute the 3rd command to include the $spuninstpath):

```
$Uniquepath = '$NtUninstallKB3002657$'
$Computer = "TestComputer"
$spuninstpath =
"\\$Computer\c$\WINDOWS\$Uniquepath\spuninst\spun
inst.exe"
$spuninstpath
```

The result of the above commands is shown in Figure 3.3.1

Figure 3.3.1 - Single Quote Example

Compare the results above with what happens when you define $Uniquepath variable using a double quote ("") as shown in the commands below. Execute each command one line at a time:

```
$Uniquepath = "$NtUninstallKB3002657$"
$Computer = "TestComputer"
$spuninstpath =
"\\$Computer\c$\WINDOWS\$Uniquepath\spuninst\spun
inst.exe"
$spuninstpath
```

The results are shown in Figure 3.3.2 below

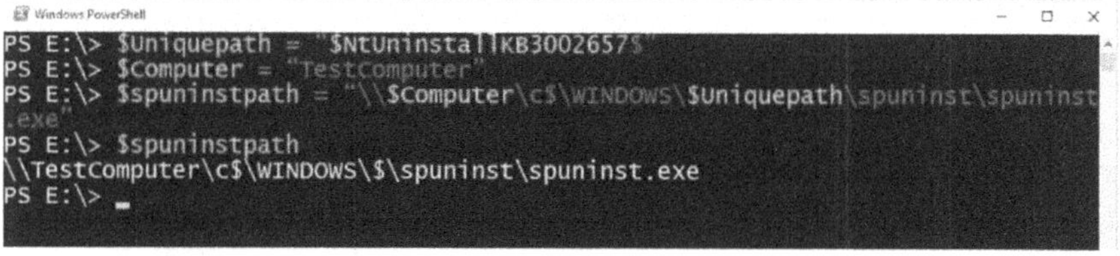

Figure 3.3.2 - Double Quote Example

Notice that PowerShell interpreted the $Uniquepath variable as a single Dollar ($) sign rather than the actual value "$NtUninstallKB3002657$". You may not fully comprehend the significance of this example but as you script in PowerShell, you may require this information. Very important to remember!

To get more information about quoting rules, execute the command below. You may also see the online help page in reference 4 at the end of the tutorial.

```
Get-Help about_quoting_rules
```

Section Summary

In this section we covered the following:

1. In Windows PowerShell, quotation marks are used to specify a literal string.
2. When defining variables, you can use single (") or Double

("") quotes. The quote mark you use will determine how PowerShell processes the variable.

3.4 PowerShell Pipelines

In PowerShell, a pipeline (|) allows you to use the output of one command as input for another command. For example, to limit the output of *Get-Process* to processes with ProcessName 'svchost', pipe the output of *Get-Process* to *Where-Object* cmdlet. See the command below:

```
Get-Process | Where-Object {$_.ProcessName -eq 'svchost'}
```

You can continue the piping to a Select-Object statement as shown below:

```
Get-Process | Where-Object {$_.ProcessName -eq 'svchost'}
| Select-Object ProcessName,Handles,Id
```

You can even pipe further to Format-Table with 'AutoSize' parameter. This fits the result into the PowerShell console window.

```
Get-Process | Where-Object {$_.ProcessName -eq 'svchost'}
| Select-Object ProcessName,Handles,Id | Format-Table -
AutoSize
```

The output of the two previous commands is shown in Figure 3.4.0

Figure 3.4.0 - PowerShell Piping

Note

Some cmdlets may not accept inputs from a pipeline. The Get-Help command provides information about parameters in a cmdlet that accept pipeline inputs.

Section Summary

In this section we covered the following:

1. In PowerShell, a pipeline (|) allows you to use the output of one command as input for another command.

Answers To Tasks In Tutorial3

Task 3.0.0

Part 1

Clear-Variable: Deletes the value of a variable.
Get-Variable: Gets the variables in the current console.
New-Variable: Creates a new variable.
Remove-Variable: Deletes a variable and its value.
Set-Variable: Sets (amends) the value of a variable. Creates the variable if one with the requested name does not exist.

Part 2
The Get-Help command will provide information about each of the cmdlets. For example Get-Help Get-Variable.

Task 3.1.0

In order to display the message "*No error message was generated*", add the code $Error.clear() right before the script. If you execute the script, it will display the message "*No error message was generated*". Reason for this?

$Error.clear() clears all errors stored in the error environment variable. Here is the amended script:

```
$Error.clear()
If (!$Error)

{Write-Host "No error message was generated"}

ElseIf ($Error)

{Write-Host ""$Error.Count" errors were generated during
the execution of this script"}
```

Downloads

1. Get-ComputerBootTime
   https://gallery.technet.microsoft.com/scriptcenter/Powe
   rShell-Function-to-572ea38e.

References And Further Reading

1. About_Variables
   https://technet.microsoft.com/en-
   us/library/hh847734.aspx
2. about_Automatic_Variables -
   https://technet.microsoft.com/en-
   us/library/hh847768.aspx
3. about_Environment_Variables
   https://technet.microsoft.com/en-
   us/library/hh847808.aspx
4. About_Quoting_Rules
   https://technet.microsoft.com/en-
   us/library/hh847740.aspx
5. about_Pipelines
   https://technet.microsoft.com/en-
   us/library/hh847902.aspx

POWERSHELL TUTORIAL 4
Introduction To Scripts And Functions

So far, you have gained significant skills about PowerShell. In this tutorial, I will introduce you to PowerShell scripts, functions and modules.

You will learn about PowerShell script extensions, and how to write them. You will also learn about PowerShell functions and their syntaxes. This tutorial will simply introduce you to functions. Volume 3 of "PowerShell Tutorial" book series covers functions and modules in details.

This tutorial will also teach you about default file locations for PowerShell. You will also learn where to place your custom scripts and functions.

Topics covered in this Tutorial will be treated under the following headings:

4.0 Introduction to Scripts
4.1 Introduction to Functions
4.2 Introduction to Modules
4.3 PowerShell File Extensions
4.4 How to Install and Use PowerShell Modules

4.0 Introduction to Scripts

A PowerShell script is a text file that contains Windows PowerShell commands. The file extension for a Windows PowerShell scripts is .ps1. Once a text file has some commands and saved with the '.ps1' file extension, Windows PowerShell will execute the file as a 'script' and run the commands in the script.

In tutorial 3, you created some scripts. Navigate to "<DriveName>\PSLab\MyScripts\Tutorial 3". If you have followed this tutorial, you should have the following files: $ErrorVariable, ClearCountErrors, EchoServerNames, Get-ComputerBootTime, MyCommandPath and WebsiteNames.

All the files have the .ps1 extension except Get-ComputerBootTime. Get-ComputerBootTime has the extension '.psm1'. We will discuss this extension later in this tutorial.

To demonstrate that these are simple text files, open PowerShell and execute the command below:

notepad "<DriveName>:\PSLab\MyScripts\Tutorial 3\ClearCountErrors.ps1"

The command opens the script ClearCountErrors.ps1 in notepad. See Figure 4.1.0 for details.

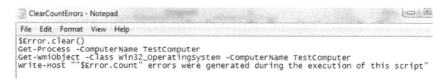

Figure 4.0.0 - Viewing a script with Notepad

PowerShell Script Editors

As already discussed, a PowerShell script is a simple plain text with PowerShell commands. In theory, you could build PowerShell scripts with notepad. Fortunately, you don't have to use notepads. There are tools called PowerShell script editors that have better functionalities.

You have already seen PowerGUI in this tutorial. It was installed during the lab installation. If you wish to download and install PowerGUI, get the link from the 'Downloads' section at the end of Tutorial 4.

Microsoft has a PowerShell script editor that comes with Windows 7 above. Microsoft's PowerShell script editor is called PowerShell ISE. ISE stands for Integrated Scripting Environment. To read more about PowerShell ISE, refer to reference 4 at the end of the tutorial.

Some benefits of using a PowerShell script editor are: command completion and suggestion, error detection and debugging. Some other benefits includes colour-coding commands and ability to execute commands within the environment and more.

I prefer PowerGUI to PowerShell ISE. You may use ISE if you want to. Actually, I recommend you try and decide your preference.

Section Summary

In this section we covered the following:

1. A PowerShell script is a text file that contains Windows PowerShell commands.
2. The file name extension for a Windows PowerShell scripts is .ps1.
3. You can build PowerShell scripts with notepad but it is better to use PowerShell script editors.
4. Two PowerShell editors were mentioned: PowerGUI (a free tool from Dell) and PowerShell ISE (a Microsoft tool).

4.1 Introduction to Functions

A PowerShell function is a list of Windows PowerShell statements with a name assigned to it. When you build a function, it executes like a normal cmdlet.

Like cmdlets, functions should be named in Verb-Noun pair and should adhere to the standard verbs that have been approved for all Windows PowerShell commands. Standard approved PowerShell verbs was covered in tutorial 1.4.

When naming your function, it is also recommended that your 'Nouns' are descriptive of the task accomplished by the function. Below is a very simple function called 'Get-CurentWorkingDirectory'.

```
Function Get-CurentWorkingDirectory { Convert-Path . }
```

This function retrieves your current working directory. Execute the previous command and then the function as shown below:

```
Get-CurentWorkingDirectory
```

Once you create a function, as seen above, you can execute it like a normal cmdlet.

Syntax of PowerShell Functions

The syntax of a function is shown below:

```
Function <function-name> {

param
(
[type]$parameter1,
[type]$parameter2,
[type]$parameter3
)

Begin {<statement list>}
Process {<statement list>}
End {<statement list>}

}
```

A function begins with the word 'Function' followed by the

name of the function. After the name of the function, every other statement is enclosed in braces ({}). In its simplest form, a function has the syntax below:

```
Function <name>
{
[type]$parameter1,
[type]$parameter2,
[type]$parameter3

<statement list>
}
```

Introducing Parameters Of PowerShell Function

As seen in the syntax above, you can define parameters for your functions. A function parameter does the same thing that a cmdlet parameter does. A parameter allows a function to accept inputs.

From the syntax, after the first open brace ({), you define parameters for the function. Then you have the three important statement blocks: 'Begin', 'Process' and 'End'.

Volume 3 of this book series covers functions in detail.

Section Summary

In this section we covered the following:

1. A PowerShell function is a list of Windows PowerShell statements with a name assigned to it.
2. The basic syntax of a function is 'Function <name> {<statements>}'.
3. You can add parameters to your functions using the reserved word 'param'.

4.2 Introduction to Modules

A Module is a package of PowerShell commands containing cmdlets, providers, functions, workflows, variables, and aliases.

To help you differentiate scripts, functions and modules; a script is a collection of PowerShell commands, a function is a named list of PowerShell statements. This means that you can easily convert any PowerShell script to a function. We can then say that the script is a subset of a function.

On the other hand, when you combine cmdlets, providers, functions, workflows, variables, and aliases into a package you create a module. So, we can say that scripts and functions are subsets of the module. This is really a simplified explanation but I hope it helps you understand the concepts.

In its simplest form, a PowerShell module is a file (.psm1) containing one or more PowerShell functions.

The script that you used to build the lab for this tutorials is a module containing different PowerShell functions. Earlier in this tutorial, we created a PowerShell called 'Get-CurentWorkingDirectory'. If we add a second function called 'Set-CurrentWorkingDirectory', we can create a module called 'CurentWorkingDirector'.

```
Function Get-CurrentWorkingDirectory { Convert-Path . }

Function Set-CurrentWorkingDirectory { Set-Location }
```

If you want to review the functions in the PSLab module (module used to build the lab for this tutorial), navigate to <DriveName>:\ PSLab\Tools\PSLab_Scripts\PSLab. Open the file PSLab.psm1 to see the functions.

Section Summary

In this section we covered the following:

1. A Module is a package of PowerShell commands containing cmdlets, providers, functions, workflows,

variables, and aliases.

2. A script is a subset of a function; functions and scripts are subsets of modules. This is a very simplified explanation!

4.3 PowerShell File Extensions

A PowerShell script file has the extension .ps1, a PowerShell module file has the extension .psm1 and a PowerShell data file has the extension .psd1.

If you open a new PowerGUI editor and click file, 'Save As', the three file types mentioned earlier will be listed in the 'Save as type' drop-down.

How to execute a PowerShell Script

You can execute a script in two ways:

1. By calling the script directly. For example, to execute the script '<DriveName>:\PSLab\MyScripts\Tutorial 3\MyCommandPath.ps1', open a PowerShell console and call it (navigate to the script and execute it as shown below).

```
'<DriveName>:\PSLab\MyScripts\Tutorial
3\MyCommandPath.ps1'
```

2. By navigating to the folder containing the script and executing it from that directory. To execute the script above by this method, first change directory to <DriveName>:\PSLab\MyScripts\Tutorial 3\'

```
Set-Location <DriveName >:\PSLab\MyScripts\Tutorial 3\'
```

Then execute the command as shown below:

```
.\MyCommandPath.ps1
```

The commands above produced the same result. They both displayed the full path to the script location. Remember to change the drive letter to the actual drive letter on your computer containing the 'PSLab' folder.

How to execute a PowerShell Function

You execute PowerShell functions same way you execute cmdlets. Simply enter the name of the function on a PowerShell console; include the function's parameters (if any) and execute the function as normal.

Earlier we created a simple PowerShell module, 'CurentWorkingDirectory'. Below is the module.

```
Function Get-CurentWorkingDirectory { Convert-Path . }

Function Set-CurentWorkingDirectory { Set-Location }
```

Copy the lines in the previous code to a new PowerGUI editor and save it as 'CurentWorkingDirectory.psm1'. Save the script in the location <DriveName >:\PSLab\MyScripts\Tutorial 4\.

To execute any of the functions in the module, simply enter the name of the function and press the enter key. If you perform this task now, you will receive error messages because the function has not been installed. This task will be completed in tutorial 4.4 (next tutorial).

Section Summary

In this section we covered the following:

1. A PowerShell script file has the extension .ps1, a PowerShell module file has the extension .psm1 and a PowerShell data file has the extension .psd1.
2. You can execute a PowerShell script by either calling the script directly or navigating to the script directly.
3. You execute PowerShell functions same way you execute cmdlets.

4.4 How To Install And Use PowerShell Modules

Beginning in Windows PowerShell 3.0, Windows PowerShell imports modules automatically the first time you execute any command in an installed module. For this to happen though, you need to have the module files in the right location. Windows PowerShell will look at certain location for modules.

Windows PowerShell stores preinstalled modules in the path: C:\Windows\System32\WindowsPowerShell\v1.0\Modules. If you navigate to this path, you will see all PowerShell modules preinstalled on your system. This path is listed when you execute the command below:

```
$env:Path
```

Also, each user has a module directory located in the path $home\Documents\WindowsPowerShell\Modules. The automatic variable, $home is usually located in C:\Users\<UserName>. To determine your $home, execute $home in your PowerShell console.

A user's PowerShell module path is not created by default and needs to be created if required. If you create or download a module, follow the steps below to install and use the module:

Step 1: Create a module directory if it does not exist. To create a module directory, execute the commands below:

```
$PSModulePath =
[environment]::getfolderpath("mydocuments") +
"\WindowsPowerShell\Modules"

If ((Test-Path $PSModulePath) -eq $false){New-Item -Path
"$PSModulePath" -ItemType Directory -Force | Out-Null }
```

Note 1

Did you notice the use of the $False automatic variable in the previous command? Can you figure out its application here?

Note 2

In the previous commands, the first command creates a variable, PSModulePath and assigns the 'My Documents' path to it. The next command, tests whether this path exists. If the path does not exist, it is created using the *New-Item* command.

Note 3

Your PowerShell module directory was created when the lab for this book was installed. The above command WILL NOT create a new module directory.

Step 2: Copy the entire module or function folder* to your module directory.

Note*

A function or module file MUST be in a folder and the folder MUST be copied to the user's module folder path.

If you copy the module or function file into the module path instead of the folder, you will not be able to import or execute the module except you specify the full path. Task 4.4.0 (later in this tutorial) illustrates this.

Step 3: Finally, before the module or function becomes available for use, it has to be imported using the Import-Module command.

Note

To put point 3 in perspective, this might not be necessary because as I mentioned earlier, from PowerShell 3.0, modules are automatically imported when you execute any command in an installed module'.

Task 4.4.0

1. Download my Get-FreeDiskSpace function (Download reference 2 - end of tutorial 4).

2. Unzip the file Get-FreeDiskSpace.zip and copy the Get-FreeDiskSpace folder to C:\Users\<UserName>\Documents\WindowsPowerShell\Modules

3. Execute the command *Import-Module Get-FreeDiskSpace*

4. To get information about the function and usage, execute the command *Get-Help Get-FreeDiskSpace -Detailed*

Scroll down the information listed by the command you executed in step 4 to see the examples.

5. To get free disk space information for the local computer, execute the command: *Get-FreeDiskSpace*

Section Summary

In this section we covered the following:

1. Beginning in Windows PowerShell 3.0, Windows PowerShell imports modules automatically the first time you execute any command in an installed module.
2. Windows PowerShell stores preinstalled modules in the path: C:\Windows\System32\WindowsPowerShell\v1.0\Modules
3. Each user has a module directory located in the path $home\Documents\WindowsPowerShell\Modules.
4. A user's PowerShell module path is not created by default and needs to be created if required.

Downloads

1. PowerGUI
   http://en.community.dell.com/techcenter/powergui/m/bits
2. Get-FreeDiskSpace
   https://gallery.technet.microsoft.com/scriptcenter/PowerShell-Function-to-cde74230

References And Further Reading

1. About_Scripts
   https://technet.microsoft.com/en-us/library/hh847841.aspx
2. About_Functions
   https://technet.microsoft.com/en-us/library/hh847829.aspx
3. About_Modules
   https://technet.microsoft.com/en-us/library/hh847804.aspx
4. Introducing the Windows PowerShell ISE
   https://technet.microsoft.com/en-us/library/dd315244.aspx

POWERSHELL TUTORIAL 5

Commenting And Breaking Scripts

When writing PowerShell scripts, it is a good practice to add comments to your scripts. Comments are not executed by PowerShell. They are usually for information purposes. Comments allow you to explain why you added a particular command in a certain way.

Comments might be for you or for any other person reviewing your scripts. This tutorial will teach you how to add comments and different ways you can do this.

This tutorial will also teach you how to break your scripts. 'Breaking' a script means to stop execution. There are so many reasons why you might want to break a script. You might test a condition and if that condition is not met, you might decide to stop executing the script.

At the end of this tutorial, you will discover reasons you might want to break your scripts and learn how to break PowerShell scripts.

You will also lean about the Escape ('backtick') character; its applications in PowerShell scripting and how to use them. Finally, this tutorial will teach you how to use comments to add help to your Functions.

Topics covered in this Tutorial will be treated under the following headings:

5.4 How to use comments to add help to your Functions

5.0 How To Add Comments To A Script

When creating a script, you might need to add comments - information that explains why you included the line of code for example.

Comments are preceded by the hash sign (#) symbol followed by the comment(s). PowerShell interprets everything after the hash sign as a comment. They will not be executed as a command or cmdlet.

Ways To Comment In PowerShell

In PowerShell, there are two ways you can add comments. You can use a single hash sign (#) for a single line comment. For example, if I want to add 'This is a comment', I will add the following lines to my PowerGUI editor *#This is a comment*.

Open an empty PowerGUI editor and enter the following lines:

```
#This is a comment
```

Notice that the hash sign and every word after it appears in green. If I want to add a lot of information as comment, it is better to enter it as shown below:

```
<#
This is a comment
Everything I add here is interpreted as comment
Nothing in this box will be executed
#>
```

On the same PowerGUI editor, beneath the first line enter the lines above exactly as it is. If you look closely, just beside the first symbol (<), notice a minimize sign. See Figure 5.0.0.

You can minimize (hide) the whole comment. After minimizing the comment block, the sign changes to a plus (+), meaning you can expand the comment. See Figure 5.0.1.

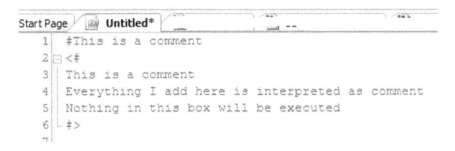

Figure 5.0.0 - Multiple Comments Maximized

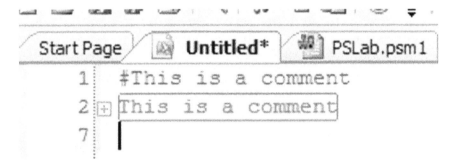

Figure 5.0.1- Multiple Comments Minimized

The symbol < #   #> is used for block/multi-line comment.

Section Summary

In this section we covered the following:

1. Comments are preceded by the hash sign (#) symbol followed by the comment(s).
2. PowerShell interprets everything after the hash sign as a comment. They will not be executed as a command or cmdlet.
3. You can use a single hash sign (#) for a single line comment.
4. The symbol, < #   #> is used for block/multi-line

comments.

5.1 Conditional Breaking Of Scripts

There are circumstances when you may need to stop a script from executing, if a condition is met. When PowerShell is executing a script and gets to the reserved word 'Break', the script will be exited.

Without breaking a script, it will continue to execute to the end of the script. You might need to break a script if the next set of commands depend on the output of a command to continue successfully.

I have used 'Break' in several scripts and functions. Typically, I use 'Break' to stop my script executing if I need to call inputs from a text file. I will normally check whether the file the user entered is a valid text file.

If user specifies a valid text file, the script will continue. Otherwise, if the user specifies an invalid text file for example a folder path, the script will exit and an error will be displayed on the console explaining why the script exited.

To illustrate my point, open the WebsiteNames.ps1 saved earlier. To open this file open PowerGUI, click *File* and select *Open*. Navigate to the location you saved the file (<DriveName>:\PSLab\MyScripts\Tutorial 3), select and open it.

Delete the $WebsiteNames variable and replace it with the following. (Change drive letter accordingly):

```
$TestFile = Get-ChildItem '<DriveName>:\PSLab\Tutorial
3\WebsiteNames.txt' -ErrorAction SilentlyContinue

If ($TestFile.Extension -eq '.txt')
{$WebsiteNames = Get-Content Get-Content $TestFile }
Else
{
Write-Host "The text file you entered is not a valid text file."
-ForegroundColor Red
Break
}
#Script amended to this point
```

Your amended script will look like Figure 5.1.0. Notice that the $WebsiteNames variable is now enclosed in the 'If' statement block. The 'If' statement simply checks whether the file's extension is a '.txt'. If true, execute the command in the $WebsiteNames variable. Else, if the file has another extension or if a folder path is specified, do not continue the script execution.

The logic behind exiting the script is simple. If you expect a text file but a user enters a folder path, your next command (Get-Content) will fail anyway. The smart thing to do is to stop executing the script if the input is not a text file. The next smart thing to do is to inform the user why the script execution stopped. That sounds like smart scripting to me!

```
#Replace <DriveName> with your actual DriveName

$TestFile = Get-ChildItem '<DriveName>:\PSLab\Tutorial 3\WebsiteNames.txt'
 -ErrorAction SilentlyContinue

If ($TestFile.Extension -eq '.txt')
{$WebsiteNames = Get-Content Get-Content $TestFile }
Else
{
Write-Host "The text file you entered is not a valid text file." -ForegroundColor Red
Break
}
#Script amended to this point
$WebsiteNames | ForEach-Object {

Test-Connection $_ -BufferSize 16 -Quiet -Count 2 |
ForEach-Object {

If ($_ -eq '$True') {

#Add further commands here

}
}
}
```

Figure 5.1.0 - Script Break Example

In the example above, it will be a very good idea to inform the user why the script stopped executing. This is achieved by adding a host message just before the 'Break'. I included a host message using the Write-Host command. This will be covered extensively in Volume 2. Before you proceed, save your updated script and close the file.

Section Summary

In this section we covered the following:

1. When PowerShell is executing a script and gets to the reserved word 'Break', the script will exit (stop executing).
2. You can use an 'IF' statement to test whether a condition is true and decide whether to exit the script.

5.2 Break Statement Examples

In this tutorial, I want to show you scripts that I have used the Break statement and why.

In tutorial 3.2, I discussed how I applied environment variables in the Get-ComputerBootTime function. In the Get-

ComputerBootTime function, I also used the Break statement. If you have not downloaded the Get-ComputerBootTime function, please download it now. Use Downloads link 1 at the end of this tutorial. Save the downloaded zip file to <DriveName >:\PSLab\MyScripts\Tutorial 5\

Extract the zip file. Open Get-ComputerBootTime.psm1 using PowerGUI. Scroll down to line 84. In tutorial 3.2, I described lines 84 to 101. Take a look at line 86. Within the 'IF' statement block, Get-ChildItem command checks the text file supplied using the 'ComputerNameFile' parameter.

Note

In the Get-ChildItem command, 'Extension' is a property of the text file. We will cover Object Properties in Tutorial 7.

If the file extension is a .txt, the command in the 'IF' statement executes. If on the other hand, the extension is not a .txt file, PowerShell displays the message in the 'Else' statement block and breaks the script.

Without the 'Break' statement, the script will execute the next command. What happens when you execute the Get-Content command on a folder path? Error message! When errors keep popping up in your script or function, it does not make for a good user experience.

Another 'Break' Statement Example

Another example I want to share with you is in a function I call 'Compare-ADGroupMember'. This function is not uploaded to the script gallery. I have a copy of the function in \PSLab\MyScripts\Tutorial 5\. The function compares two Active Directory Groups to find members that are in both groups.

Navigate to the path above and open Compare-ADGroupMember.psm1 in PowerGUI. Between lines 31 and 46, I used the 'Break' statement twice. Scroll back to line 7.

Notice the 'param' statement? I have two parameters called 'GroupNameA' and 'GroupNameB'.

When a user executes the Compare-ADGroupMember function, the user supplies these two parameters. My first task is to search for the group names in Active Directory and confirm that they are valid groups. If any of the group is invalid, I will break the script because there will be no groups to compare!

In line 31, I execute the Get-ADGroupMember on 'GroupNameA'. The command extracts the members of the group and returns their SamAccountNames. But most importantly, I enclosed the command in a 'Try' 'Catch'. If there are any exceptions (errors, etc), the command within the 'Catch' statement executes.

For instance, if the Get-ADGroupMember command does not find the group with the supplied 'Identity', it returns an error (exception). Once this happens, the exception message is displayed and the 'Break' statement is executed.

On the other hand, if the Get-ADGroupMember command executes without any exception (errors), the other parts of the script continues. This same logic applies to the command on line 40.

Note

Volume 3 covers Error management and handling; including 'Try', 'Catch' statement blocks.

Section Summary

In this section we covered the following:

1. You saw two practical applications of the 'Break' statement
2. If you intend to write something to host, it is very important to do it before the 'Break' statement.

5.3 How To Use The Escape (Backtick) Character

As you script, you will discover that sometimes a line of code might become too long to stay in a single line. In such circumstances, you may decide to move parts of the command to the next line. The backtick character (`) is used to accomplish this. The backtick character is the key just below Esc key on your keyboard.

In Windows PowerShell, the escape character is the backtick (`). This character can be used to indicate a literal, to indicate line continuation, and to indicate special characters. The escape character tells Windows PowerShell that the command continues on the next line.

Let's add a line break to the first command in the WebsiteNames.ps1 script. Open the WebsiteNames.ps1 script and amend the first line as follows:

After the Get-ChildItem cmdlet, leave a single space followed by a backtick (`) character then press enter. Just before -ErrorAction, enter another backtick (`) character then press enter. The previous single line command will now appear as shown below:

```
$TestFile = Get-ChildItem `
'<DriveName>:\PSLab\Tutorial 3\WebsiteNames.txt' `
-ErrorAction SilentlyContinue
```

Your amended script should look like Figure 5.3.0. Compare this with Figure 5.1.0 which has the same script without the backtick (`) character.

```
Start Page    WebsiteNames.ps1
 1  #Replace <DriveName> with your actual DriveName
 2
 3  $TestFile = Get-ChildItem
 4  '<DriveName>:\PSLab\Tutorial 3\WebsiteNames.txt'
 5  -ErrorAction SilentlyContinue
 6
 7  If ($TestFile.Extension -eq '.txt')
 8  {$WebsiteNames = Get-Content Get-Content $TestFile }
 9  Else
10  {
11  Write-Host "The text file you entered is not a valid text file." -ForegroundColor Red
12  Break
13  }
14  #Script amended to this point
15  $WebsiteNames | ForEach-Object {
16
17  Test-Connection $_ -Buffersize 16 -Quiet -Count 2 |
18  ForEach-Object {
19
20  If ($_ -eq '$True') {
21
22  #Add further commands here
23
24  }
25  }
```

Figure 5.3.0 - Script Backtick Example

As you can see, using the 'backtick' character makes your scripting neater. This is very simple but could make a big difference in complex scripts.

Note

For more on how to use the escape (backtick) character, see reference 5 at the end of this tutorial.

Section Summary

In this section we covered the following:

1. In Windows PowerShell, the escape character is the backtick (`).
2. The escape character tells Windows PowerShell that the command continues on the next line.

5.4 How To Use Comments To Add Help To Functions

In tutorial 4.1, we discussed PowerShell functions. In tutorial 1, we saw how the Get-Help command can provide information about cmdlets.

In tutorial 5.0, we said that the symbol <#   #> is used for block/multi-line comment. This same symbols can be used to add help information to your functions.

This tutorial will teach you how to add help information to your functions. When you add help to your function, when a user executes 'Get-Hell Your-Function-Name', the help information is displayed for the user.

As discussed in In tutorial 4.1, the simplified form of a function's syntax is shown below:

```
Function <name>
{
[type]$parameter1,
[type]$parameter2,
[type]$parameter3

<statement list>
 }
```

When we discussed the Get-Help command, we said that the help information is displayed under the following sections: NAME, SYNOPSIS, SYNTAX, DESCRIPTION, RELATED LINKS and REMARKS.

To proceed with this tutorial, we will add help information to our WebsiteNames script. First, let's convert the script to a function. We will call the new function, Get-WebsiteIPs. From PowerGUI, open WebsiteNames.ps1 from \PSLab\MyScripts\Tutorial 3\. Modify the script as shown below and save it as Get-WebsiteIPs.psm1. Save Get-WebsiteIPs.psm1 in \PSLab\MyScripts\Tutorial 5\Get-WebsiteIPs\.

```
Function Get-WebsiteIPs {

    #Replace <DriveName> with your actual DriveName

    $TestFile = Get-ChildItem `
    '<DriveName>:\PSLab\Tutorial 3\WebsiteNames.txt' `
    -ErrorAction SilentlyContinue

    If ($TestFile.Extension -eq '.txt')
    {$WebsiteNames = Get-Content Get-Content $TestFile }
    Else
    {
    Write-Host "The text file you entered is not a valid text
file." -ForegroundColor Red
    Break
    }
    #Script amended to this point
    $WebsiteNames | ForEach-Object {

    Test-Connection $_ -BufferSize 16 -Quiet -Count 2 |
    ForEach-Object {

    If ($_ -eq '$True') {

    #Add further commands here

    }
    }

    }

}
```

The only change to the script is that I enclosed the previous
script in the function loop - 'Function Get-WebsiteIPs {   }'.
See my updated script in Figure 5.4.0.

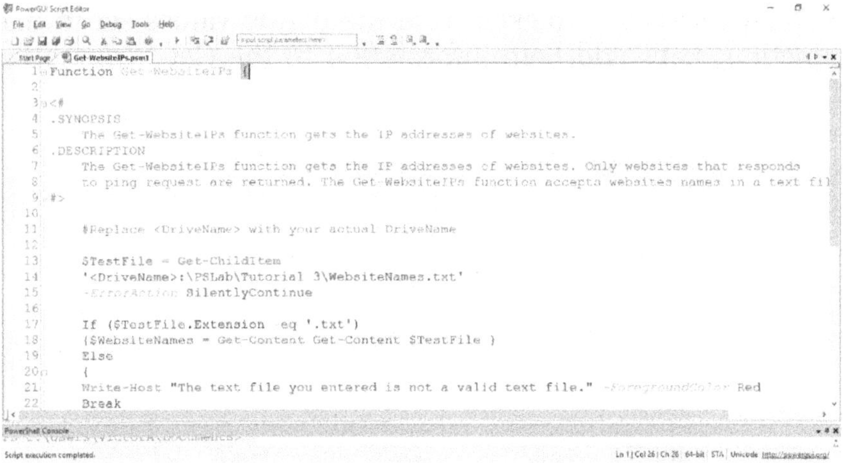

Figure 5.4.0 - Function Get-WebsiteIPs (Illustration only, portions of the script are hidden)

As a reminder, lets execute the Get-Help command to see how the help information is displayed.

```
Get-Help -Name Get-Command
```

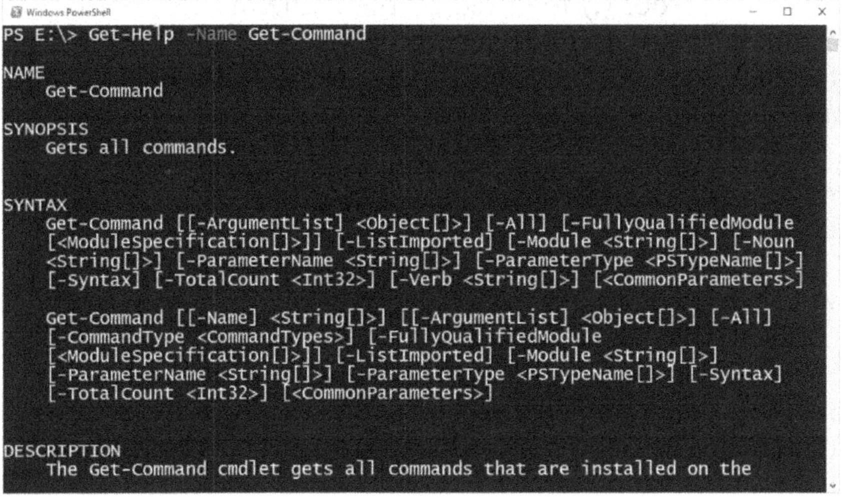

Figure 5.4.1 - Get-Help -Name Get-Command (Result)

The NAME section picks the function name automatically.

SYNTAX section is picked from the param values set in the function. Let's add help information to the Get-WebsiteIPs function.

Step 1: Just after the opening bracket '{', enter a multi-comment symbol - <# #>. See Figure 5.4.2 for details.

```
Start Page   Get-WebsiteIPs.psm1*
 1 Function Get-WebsiteIPs  {
 2
 3 <#
 4 |
 5 #>
 6
 7      #Replace <DriveName> with your actual DriveName
 8
 9      $TestFile = Get-ChildItem
10      '<DriveName>:\PSLab\Tutorial 3\WebsiteNames.txt'
11      -ErrorAction SilentlyContinue
12
```

Figure 5.4.2 - Add Comment-based help (1) (Illustrations only)

Step 2: Add the different help sections. To add a section, start with a dot (.) followed by the name of the section. For example '.SYNOPSIS'. Beneath the section, add information for that section. See Figure 5.4.3 for details. Below is the additional information included in the script:

```
<#
.SYNOPSIS
    The Get-WebsiteIPs function gets the IP addresses of
websites.
.DESCRIPTION
    The Get-WebsiteIPs function gets the IP addresses of
websites. Only websites that responds to ping request are
returned. The Get-WebsiteIPs function accepts websites
names in a text file.
#>
```

```
tart Page   Get-WebsiteIPs.psm1                                                                          ◄ ▷ ▾ ✕
 1  Function Get-WebsiteIPs {
 2
 3  <#
 4  .SYNOPSIS
 5      The Get-WebsiteIPs function gets the IP addresses of websites.
 6  .DESCRIPTION
 7      The Get-WebsiteIPs function gets the IP addresses of websites. Only websites that responds
 8      to ping request are returned. The Get-WebsiteIPs function accepts websites names in a text fil
 9  #>
10
11      #Replace <DriveName> with your actual DriveName
12  |
13      $TestFile = Get-ChildItem
14      '<DriveName>:\PSLab\Tutorial 3\WebsiteNames.txt'
15      -ErrorAction SilentlyContinue
1
```

Figure 5.4.3 - Add Comment-based help (2) (Illustrations only)

To see the result of the comment-based help, copy the Get-WebsiteIPs folder to \Documents\WindowsPowerShell\Modules\.

Note

To get the full path to your module folder, execute the command: [environment]::getfolderpath("mydocuments") + "\WindowsPowerShell\Modules"

Open a PowerShell console and execute the command below:

Get-Help Get-WebsiteIPs -Detailed

The result is shown in Figure 5.4.4

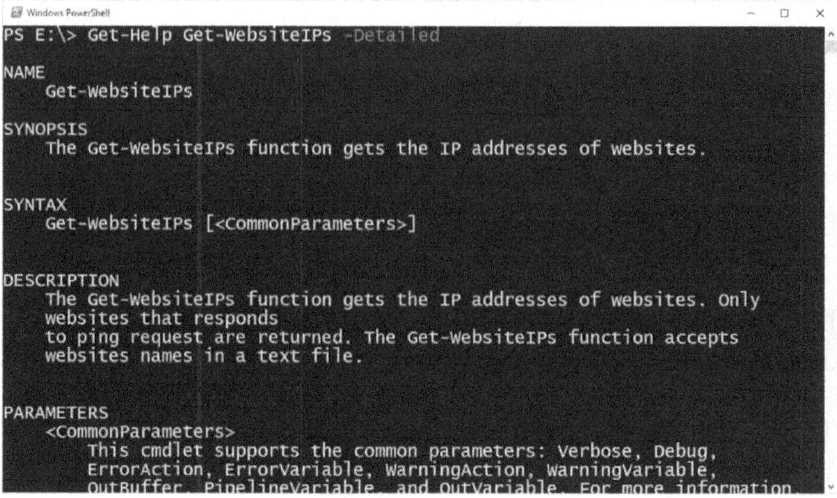

Figure 5.4.4 - Get-Help Get-WebsiteIPs -Detailed

Compare the result of Figure 5.4.4 with Figure 5.4.3. See any similarities? The information on the SYNOPSIS and DESCRIPTION sections of the Get-Help result is exactly the same as what you entered in the help section of the function. You have just created your first function and added help information!

Section Summary

In this section we covered the following:

1. The symbol <#   #> is used to add block/multi-line comments in scripts and functions.
2. This same symbol is used to add comment-based help in functions.
3. To add a comment-based help, within the '<#   #>' block, enter a dot, followed by the name of the section.

Downloads

1. Get-ComputerBootTime
   https://gallery.technet.microsoft.com/PowerShell-Function-to-572ea38e.

References And Further Reading

1. About_Break
   https://technet.microsoft.com/en-us/library/hh847873.aspx
2. About_Continue
   https://technet.microsoft.com/en-us/library/hh847821.aspx
3. About_Return
   https://technet.microsoft.com/en-us/library/hh847760.aspx
4. About_Comment_Based_Help
   https://technet.microsoft.com/en-us/library/hh847834.aspx
5. About_Escape_Characters
   https://technet.microsoft.com/en-us/library/hh847755.aspx

VICTOR ASHIEDU

POWERSHELL TUTORIAL 6

PowerShell Operators

As you progress with PowerShell, you will need to perform some simple arithmetic operations. You will also definitely need to perform some comparison operations. When performing arithmetic and comparison operations you will almost certainly require a third set of operators - logical operators.

This tutorial will introduce you to PowerShell operators. These operators help you to perform comparisons, simple calculations and more.

Topics covered in this Tutorial will be treated under the following headings:

6.0 Comparison Operators
6.1 Arithmetic and Logical Operators
6.2 Split and Join Operators
6.3 Redirection and Assignment Operators
6.4 Special Operators

6.0 Comparison Operations

Let's start this section by executing the command below:

```
Get-WmiObject win32_logicaldisk
```

The result of the previous command is shown in Figure 6.0.0. This has produced a report about drive partitions on my computer but the report doesn't make much sense. In this section, we will commence the creation of a script that reports free disk space on a computer.

```
PS C:\> Get-WmiObject win32_logicaldisk


DeviceID      : C:
DriveType     : 3
ProviderName  :
FreeSpace     : 235682959360
Size          : 319743324160
VolumeName    : OSDisk

DeviceID      : E:
DriveType     : 5
ProviderName  :
FreeSpace     :
Size          :
VolumeName    :

DeviceID      : F:
DriveType     : 5
ProviderName  :
FreeSpace     :
Size          :
VolumeName    :
```

Figure 6.0.0 - Get-WmiObject win32_logicaldisk

Comparison operators allow you specify conditions for comparing object values with the aim of filtering results to match specified patterns.

Take another look at Figure 6.0.0; notice that DriveID 'E' and 'F' has a DriveType with a value of '5'. This is different from the DriveType for 'C'. Drive 'E' and 'F' are DVD drives.

When creating a disk report, I may not wish to return DVD drives. If we apply a comparison operator to the previous command, we will return drives with DriveType equals '3'. To achieve this, we will pipe the command in Figure 6.0.0 to a Where-Object command as shown below:

Get-WmiObject win32_logicaldisk | Where-Object
{$_.DriveType -eq '3'}

Do you remember our automatic variable, '$_'? Notice how it was used with the 'DriveType' property? In this section, we are focusing on the comparison operator 'eq' - 'Equal To'. The command above will return the results shown in Figure 6.0.1.

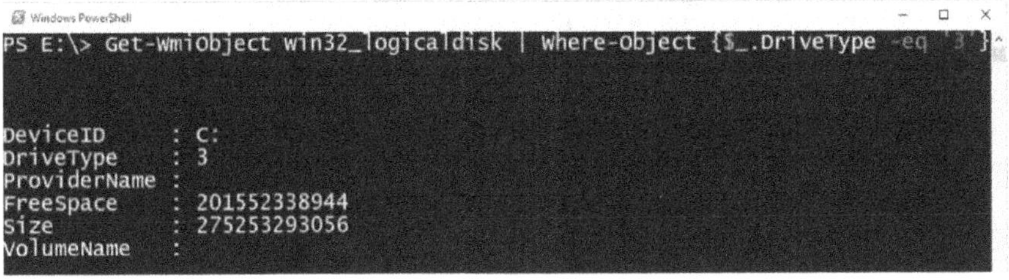

Figure 6.0.1 - Get-WmiObject win32_logicaldisk ('eq')

Let's use two other comparison operators ('le' - 'Less Than or Equal To') and -match (means what is says) in the same command as shown below:

Get-WmiObject win32_logicaldisk | Where-Object
{$_.DriveType -le '3'}

Get-WmiObject win32_logicaldisk | Where-Object
{$_.DriveType -match '3'}

The two commands produced same result as the previous command.

Note
To read more about comparison operators, see reference 2 (About_Comparison_Operators) at the end of the tutorial.

Before we expand our disk report script further, let's save the script. Open a new PowerGUI editor and enter the command below:

```
Get-WmiObject win32_logicaldisk | Where-Object
{$_.DriveType -eq '3'}
```

Save the file in the location \PSLab\MyScripts\Tutorial 6\Get-FreeDiskSpace.psm1.

Section Summary

In this section we covered the following:

1. Comparison operators allow you specify conditions for comparing object values with the aim of filtering results to match specified patterns.

6.1 Arithmetic And Logical Operation

Open the script you saved in the previous tutorial (Get-FreeDiskSpace.psm1) in PowerGUI editor. Amend it as shown in the commands below:

```
Get-WmiObject win32_logicaldisk | Where-Object
{$_.DriveType -eq '3' -and ($_.FreeSpace/$_.Size) -ge '0.1' }
```

In the last command, I introduced two more operators. Can you spot them? The command contains an arithmetic operator '/' and a logical operator 'and'. The 'and' operator combines the two conditions to determine the result and requires that conditions on either side of the operator must be met.

If we were to use another common logical operator 'or', we would have a different result. Unlike the 'and' operator, the 'or' operator requires that any condition on either side of the operator is met. Let's give the 'or' operator a shot. Add the command below to your script:

```
Get-WmiObject win32_logicaldisk | `
```

```
Where-Object {$_.DriveType -eq '3' -or
($_.FreeSpace/$_.Size) -ge '0.1' }
```

Your script will look like this:

```
Get-WmiObject win32_logicaldisk | `
Where-Object {$_.DriveType -eq '3' -and
($_.FreeSpace/$_.Size) -ge '0.1' }

Get-WmiObject win32_logicaldisk | `
Where-Object {$_.DriveType -eq '3' -or
($_.FreeSpace/$_.Size) -ge '0.1' }
```

Highlight the whole text in your PowerGUI editor, right-click and select 'execute selection'. The second command throws the error messages *"Attempted to divide by zero"* as shown in Figure 6.1.0.

Why did the second command throw this error? The answer lies in the 'or' operator. The 'or' logical operator requires that the first or the second condition needed to be true to return a result.

This meant that the command attempted to return the DVD drive and since the DVD drive has null values for 'FreeSpace' and 'Size', attempting to divide $_.FreeSpace by $_.Size (null values), returned an error. You cannot divide a value with zero.

Note

The 'and' operator requires that **BOTH** conditions on either side of the operator be met; on the other hand, the 'or' operator requires that **ANY** of the conditions on either side of the operator be met.

Figure 6.1.0 - 'and', 'or' logical operators (errors)

Having demonstrated the difference between the 'and' and the 'or' logical operators, let's return to our original script. Delete the second command with the 'or' operator and ensure that your script looks like this:

```
Get-WmiObject win32_logicaldisk | Where-Object
{$_.DriveType -eq '3' -and ($_.FreeSpace/$_.Size) -ge '0.1' }
```

The command requested to find all disk drives with drive type '3' and percentage free space "greater than or equal to" 10%.

Let's see how I came up with this theory. Refer to Figure 6.0.0. In this figure, 'FreeSpace' is 235666472960 Bytes while Size equals 319743324160 Bytes. If you divide

235666472960 by 319743324160, the result is 0.7370489237863561. This is the fraction of the disk that is free. To get the value in percentage, multiply 0.7370489237863561 by 100. That gives us 73.70% (approximately).

So, what our previous command did was to first determine that a particular drive was of DriveType '3'. If this is true, it then divides the 'FreeSpace' value of the drive by its 'Size' value; then compared the result with '0.1'.

If 'FreeSpace/Size' is "greater than or equal to" 0.1, as shown in our manual example (0.74 is definitely greater than 0.1!), the drive is returned, otherwise, the drive is not returned. As this script span out, I believe you are beginning to see how helpful this tool can be to a Systems Administrator?

Note

The Get-WmiObject win32_logicaldisk command returns disk sizes in Bytes. In Volume 2, you will learn how to convert these values into MB and GB as well as how to compute percentages.

Arithmetic operators calculate numeric values (add, subtract, multiply, or divide) while Logical operators connect expressions and statements. The arithmetic operator '/' was used in our previous command to calculate a percentage value.

Logical operators allow you to test multiple conditions in a single command. In our previous command, the 'and' logical operator connected the statements "$_.DriveType -eq '3'" and "($_.FreeSpace/$_.Size) -ge '0.1'". Without the use of the 'and' operator, we would have had to execute two separate commands to achieve the same objective.

Task 6.0.0

The command *Get-ChildItem "C:\Google Drive\PSLab"*, returned the result shown in Figure 6.1.1. You want to return only the folder called 'Tool's. How would you amend the command to achieve your aim?

How will the command change if you want to return the folders 'Tools' and 'MyScripts'? See answers at the end of the tutorial.

```
PS C:\> Get-ChildItem "C:\Google Drive\PSLab"

    Directory: C:\Google Drive\PSLab

Mode                LastWriteTime         Length Name
----                -------------         ------ ----
d-----        28/09/2015     08:59                MyScripts
d-----        21/04/2015     10:14                Tools
d-----        24/09/2015     15:43                Tutorial 1
d-----        28/05/2015     15:48                Tutorial 2
d-----        24/09/2015     15:43                Tutorial 3
```

Figure 6.1.1 - Get-ChildItem (Task 6.0.0)

Section Summary

In this section we covered the following:

1. Arithmetic operators calculate numeric values (add, subtract, multiply, or divide), while Logical operators connect expressions and statements.
2. Logical operators allow you to test multiple conditions in a single command.

6.2 Split and Join Operators

I built a PowerShell function, Update-ADUsers that updates missing attributes of Active Directory users using values from a CSV file. One of the attributes updated by this function is the 'manager' attribute.

Task 6.2.0

Download the Update-ADUsers function using the link found in Downloads reference 1 - end of the tutorial. Save the zip file to \PSLab\MyScripts\Tutorial 6. Unzip Update-ADUsers.zip and open Update-ADUsers.psm1 in your PowerGUI.

As I mentioned earlier, the script that executes the Update-ADUsers function updates an Active Directory user's attributes using values in a CSV file. The 'Manager' column in the CSV file is provided in 'FirstName LastName' format. To be able to update a user's 'Manager' attribute in Active Directory, the manager name must be converted to DistinguishedName (DN) format.

To convert the manager's name from 'FirstName LastName' to DistinguishedName format, I had to execute the Get-ADUser command in lines 124-127. Open Update-ADUsers function in PowerGUI, and scroll to line 124. When I executed the Get-ADUser command as shown below, some of the managers were not found in Active Directory. Let's execute a similar command in our lab:

> Get-ADUser -Server 10.0.0.2 -Filter {name -like 'test*'} - Credential PSLab.local\administrator

This command returns results in our lab because we have users with names 'Test1 User1', 'Test2 User2', and so on. This was not the case when I executed the command in one of my production domains. It turns out that some of the names in my production domain were in 'FirstName LastName', others were in 'LastName FirstName' format.

I used the 'Split' operator to resolve the problem. Refer to the Update-ADUsers function in your PowerGUI and examine lines 107 to 119. These lines of code achieved the following:

Step 1: Split the manager name field from the CSV file into

'FirstName' and 'LastName'. To experience the power of split operator, execute the commands:

```
$ManagerFirstname ='Test1 User1'.Split("")[0]

$ManagerLastname ='Test1 User1'.Split("")[-1]
```

The result of the first command is Test1, and the result of the second is User1. These results are stored in the variables, $ManagerFirstname and $ManagerLastname respectively. We have effectively 'split' the names into two parts (substrings) - 'FirstName' and 'LastName'!

Step 2: Next, I defined three variables ($ManagerDN1, $ManagerDN2 and $ManagerDN3) using the arithmetic operator '+' to produce different combinations of potential names as they may likely appear in Active Directory. This is demonstrated by the commands below:

```
$ManagerDN1 = "$ManagerFirstname" +
"$ManagerLastname"

$ManagerDN2 = "$ManagerFirstname" + "
$ManagerLastname"

$ManagerDN3 = "$ManagerLastname" +
"$ManagerFirstname"
```

Note

If you look closely at these commands, the second command has a space just before the $ManagerLastname variable (unfortunately, if you are reading this book in Kindle, this may not be properly formatted).

To appreciate the difference between the first and the second command, execute $ManagerDN1 and $ManagerDN2

Step 3: In the last part of the code, I executed the Get-ADUser command using the various name combinations obtained in step 2 above as shown in the 'Filter' parameter. Let's execute a similar command in our lab:

Get-ADUser -Server 10.0.0.2 -Filter {(name -like $ManagerDN1) -or (name -like $ManagerDN2) -or (name -like $ManagerDN3)} -Credential PSLab.local\administrator

The last command searches for any user with name LIKE 'Test1User1' OR name LIKE 'Test1 User1' OR name LIKE 'User1Test1'. The result of the command is shown in Figure 6.2.0.

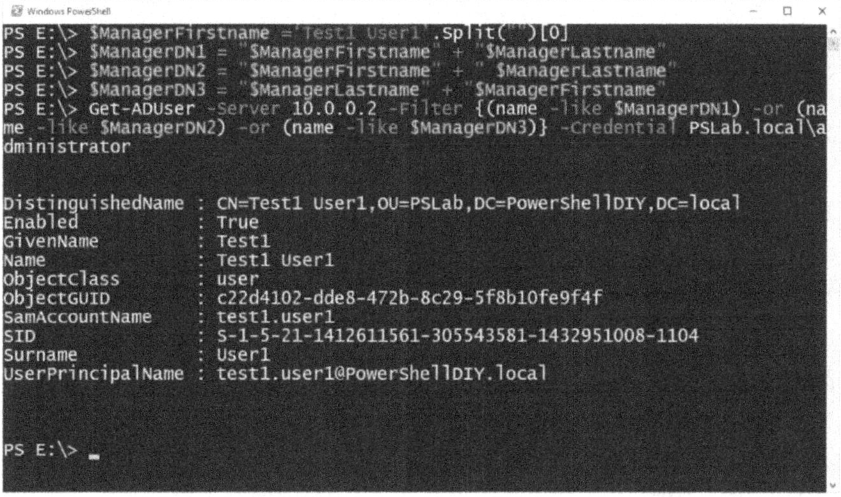

Figure 6.2.0 - Split Operator Example

While the 'Split' operator breaks one or more strings into substrings (parts), the 'Join' operator links a set of strings into a single string.

We have seen an example of how the 'Split' operator may be used. Let's examine some applications of the 'Join' operator. Execute the following commands, one line at a time on your PowerShell console (Each box represents a complete set of commands):

```
$FirstName = "Test1"

$LastName = "User1"

-Join ("$FirstName", " $LastName")
```

```
$Name = "Test1 User1"

(-Split $Name) -join ", "
```

```
$groupnames = Get-Content
"<DriveName>:\PSLab\Tutorial 6\Joinoperator.txt"

$groupnames

(-split $groupnames) -join ", "
```

The result of the last set of commands is shown in Figure 6.2.1. You will see more applications of the 'Join' operator in Volume 2 after you have learnt how to create hash tables and custom labels.

Info

The text file Joinoperator.txt contains a list of names called Group1 to Group27. The first command retrieved the content of the text file into a variable, 'groupnames'.

The second command displayed the file content (stored in the variable). In the third command, the 'Split' operator separated the groups into substrings and finally the 'Join' operator added a comma (,) between each group name.

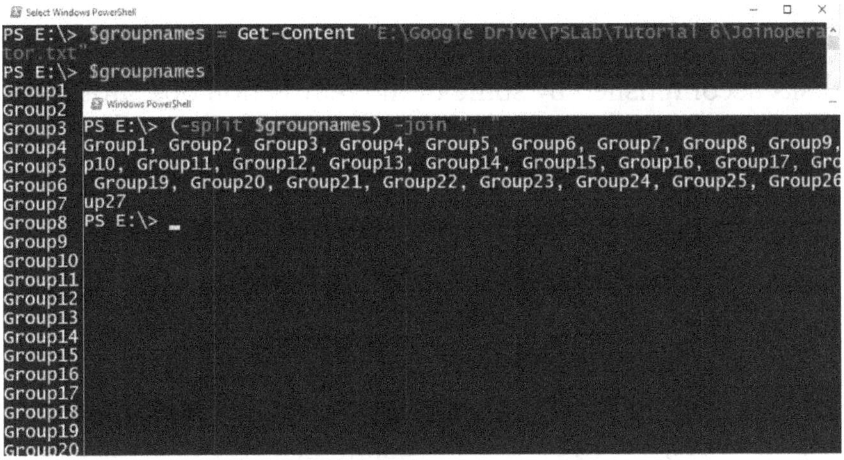

Figure 6.2.1 - Joint, Split Operator example

Note

Some results of the previous command are not shown in Figure 6.2.1. The result of the last command (shown on the right) is merged with the result of the first two commands.

Info

To read more about operators, refer to the link in reference number 1 at the end of this tutorial.

Section Summary

In this section we covered the following:

1. the 'Split' operator breaks one or more strings into substrings (parts).
2. the 'Join' operator links a set of strings into a single string.

6.3 Redirection and Assignment Operators

Redirection operators are used to send the output of a command or expression to a text file. Table 6.3.0 lists the common redirection operators and what they are used for. For more information about redirection operators, see references 1 and 7 at the end of the tutorial.

Out-File and Add-Content cmdlets can perform some of the tasks accomplished by some of the redirection operators. For instance, Out-File sends output to a specified text file while Out-File with 'Append' parameter   Appends output to a specified file.

S/N	Operator	What it does
1	>	Sends output to a specified file.
2	>>	Appends output to a specified file
3	2>	Sends errors to a specified file.
4	2>>	Appends errors to a specified file.
5	2>&1	Sends errors (2) and success output (1) to the success output stream.

Table 6.3.0 - Common redirection operators

In tutorial 1.1, you created a file called Outfile.txt. If you recollect, we used the Add-Content cmdlet to add additional contents to the file. Let's perform a similar task using redirection operators. Execute the commands below:

"Redirection Operator Test; new input to the text file" >
"<DriveName>\PSLab\Tutorial 6\RO.txt"

Let's append a second line to the text file RO.txt

"Redirection Operator Test; second line to the text file" >>
"<DriveName>\PSLab\Tutorial 6\RO.txt"

Open RO.txt and confirm that the two lines are on the text file.

Finally, let's see how '2>' and '2>>' operators send and append errors to a text file. Execute the commands below:

```
Get-Process noname 2> "<DriveName>\PSLab\Tutorial 6\Errors.txt"
```

The command above should generate an error because 'noname' is not the name of a process. The '2>' operator sent the error to the text file. To see the error details open the text file. Let's now append a second error into the same text file. Execute the command below:

```
Get-Process NewName 2>> "<DriveName>\PSLab\Tutorial 6\Errors.txt"
```

This command appends a second error beneath the first error. When scripting, you can use this method to log errors to a text file.

Assignment Operators

When we discussed variables earlier in this book, we used assignment operators. Assignment operators assign one or more values to a variable. Assignment operators can also perform numeric operations. Let's take some examples. First create a variable called AOp.

```
$AOp = 5
```

In the previous command, '=' is an assignment operator. It assigned the value of '5' to the variable AOp.

Next, let's add another value to the existing value in the variable:

```
$AOp += 2
```

The second command adds 2 to 5, making the value of the variable 7. To see the result, execute the variable after the second command.

This can be applied in a 'while' loop. Let's say you create a variable and assign it an initial value of '1'. You can use the '+=' operator to add a specific value to the current value of the variable. You can then loop through the values with the 'while' loop until you reached a desired value.

Section Summary

In this section we covered the following:

1. Redirection operators are used to send the output of a command or expression to a text file.
2. Assignment operators assign one or more values to a variable. Assignment operators can also perform numeric operations.

6.4 Special Operators

Special Operators perform tasks that cannot be performed by the other types of operators. One very important special operator is the array subexpression operator, '@( )'. Array subexpression operator returns the result of one or more statements as an array.

An array is a data structure that is designed to store a collection of items. You can create an array by assigning values to a variable as shown below:

```
$ArrayOp = "Group1", "Group2"
```

Sometimes, you may want to return the result of a command in an array. For example to return *Get-WMIObject win32_logicalDisk* in an array, enclose it in the Array subexpression special operator, '@( )'.

```
@(Get-WMIObject win32_logicalDisk)
```

An array separate the results of a command into a collection of items. This allows you to loop through the collection and perform a specific task on each item if you wanted to.

To learn more about operators, see references at the end of the tutorial.

Section Summary

In this section we covered the following:

1. Special Operators perform tasks that cannot be performed by the other types of operators.

Downloads

1. Update-ADUsers
   https://gallery.technet.microsoft.com/scriptcenter/Powe
   rShell-Function-to-e1eb6441

Answers To Tasks In Tutorial 6

Task 6.0.0

To return 'Tools' folder, pipe the result to Where-Object {$_.Name -eq 'Tools'} as shown below:

```
Where-Object {$_.Name -eq 'Tools'}
```

To return the folders 'Tools' and 'MyScripts', amend the script as shown below:

```
Get-ChildItem "C:\Google Drive\PSLab" | Where-Object
{$_.Name -eq 'Tools' -or $_.Name -eq 'MyScripts'}
```

References And Further Reading

2. About_Operators
   https://msdn.microsoft.com/en-
   us/library/ms714428%28v=vs.85%29.aspx?f=255&MSP

PError=-2147217396
3. About_Comparison_Operators
   https://technet.microsoft.com/en-us/library/hh847759.aspx
4. About_Arithmetic_Operators
   https://technet.microsoft.com/en-us/library/hh848303.aspx
5. About_Logical_Operators
   https://technet.microsoft.com/en-us/library/hh847789.aspx
6. About_Split
   https://technet.microsoft.com/en-us/library/hh847811.aspx
7. About_Join
   https://technet.microsoft.com/en-us/library/hh847757.aspx
8. About_Redirection
   https://technet.microsoft.com/en-us/library/hh847746.aspx
9. About_Type_Operators
   https://technet.microsoft.com/en-us/library/hh847763.aspx
10. About_Assignment_Operators
    https://technet.microsoft.com/en-us/library/hh847875.aspx
11. About_Arrays
    https://technet.microsoft.com/en-gb/library/hh847882.aspx

POWERSHELL TUTORIAL
7
Introduction To Object Properties

Understanding object properties is very important to your PowerShell scripting. Without the knowledge of object properties and how to manipulate them, you may not have a good grasps of PowerShell scripting.

In the last tutorial of this volume, you will learn about object properties and how to access and manipulate the them. You will learn about object members and how to use them. You will also learn the difference between object properties and methods.

Topics covered in this Tutorial will be treated under the following headings:

7.0 What are Object Properties?
7.1 How to Access Object Properties Using Variables
7.2 Member Types and Applications
7.3 Exploring The Get-Member Cmdlet
7.4 How to use Objects in Pipelines

7.0 What Are Object Properties?

An object is a collection of data that represents an item. An object is made up of three types of data: the objects type, its methods, and its properties. Let's bring this definition to life by executing the command below:

```
Get-ChildItem "<DriveLetter>:\PSLab\Tutorial
6\Joinoperator.txt" | Get-Member
```

You are familiar with the first part of the command (command before the pipeline) but may not be familiar with the second. See whether you can make anything out of the result in Figure 7.0.0.

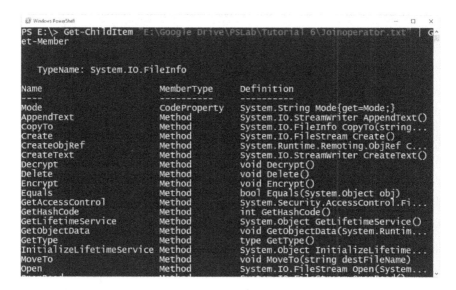

Figure 7.0.0 - Object Properties and Methods (portions of the result are not shown)

Refer to Figure 7.0.0 , if you look right on top of the result, you will see 'TypeName: System.IO.FileInfo". This is the object type. FileInfo, represents a file. To see two other object types, execute the following commands one line at a time:

Get-Process | Get-Member

Get-ChildItem "<DriveLetter>:\PSLab" | Get-Member

In the first command the TypeName is 'System.Diagnostics.Process' while the second command has a TypeName of 'System.IO.DirectoryInfo'. An object that represents a process is a 'Process' object while an object that represents a folder or directory is a 'DirectoryInfo' object.

Refer to Figure 7.0.0 once more. Notice that the command

result has a column called 'MemberType'. This column has MemberType called 'Method'. It also has another MemberType called 'Property' or variant of 'Property'.

An object's properties store information about the object; its methods are actions you can perform on the object. In other words, objects properties store data about the object, and it's methods let you change the object.

Object Properties and Methods

An object's properties are like the components of the object. For instance a file has the following properties: Name, Extension, LastWriteTime, Length and more. You will expect to see a different set of properties for a Process. A Process has the following properties:ProcessName, Id (Process ID), MachineName (Computer running the process) and more.

Using the Get-Member cmdlet to view the full list of an object's properties and methods is very useful. This helps you understand what property to return in a report and how to manipulate the object using its methods.

For you to appreciate how important it is to have a way to find an object's property, execute the command below:

```
Get-Content "<DriveLetter>:\PSLab\Tutorial 7\Groups.txt"
```

The command produces the content of the text file. If this is all we know about this file, we cannot do more than use the content as input to another command. The command below will reveal that there is more we can accomplish with this text file. Compare the output of the previous command and that of the command below in Figure 7.0.1.

```
Get-Content "<DriveLetter>:\PSLab\Tutorial 7\Groups.txt"|
`
Get-Member
```

In 7.0.1, I merged the results of the two commands into one image. On the right hand side of Figure 7.0.1, notice that there is a property called 'Length' (not shown in the image). You also notice that there are multiple 'methods'. Let's see what information the property, 'Length' holds. We can utilize the command completion capabilities of PowerShell.

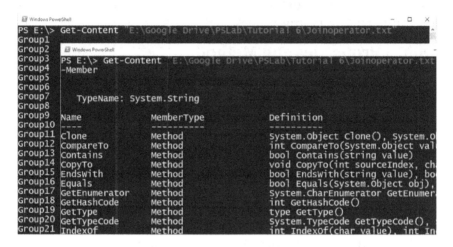

Figure 7.0.1 - Get-Content properties example

Enter the command below in your PowerShell console and press the Tab key:

```
(Get-Content "<DriveLetter>:\PSLab\Tutorial
7\Groups.txt").Len
```

The command completes as shown below:

```
(Get-Content "<DriveLetter>:\PSLab\Tutorial
7\Groups.txt").Length
```

A few things to note:

1. To access the property or method of an object, enclose the object in bracket (), followed by a dot (.) then the property or method.

2. To access a method, additional actions may be required (more on this later in this tutorial).
3. The object can be stored in a variable and accessed via the variable (more on this later in this tutorial).
4. The properties or methods of the object can be listed using the following methods:
   a. Get-Member
   b. Command completion
   c. Scripting editor like PowerGUI

I have covered 4.a and 4.b in this tutorial. 4.c is covered in "PowerShell Tutorial: Volume 2". Going back to the previous command, execute the command as shown below:

```
(Get-Content "<DriveLetter>:\PSLab\Tutorial 7\Groups.txt").Length
```

The command above returns a value of 27. Open the text file and count the number of items listed. Notice that there 27 items? So, you can easily count values in a text file using this approach.

There are some other useful properties of a text file that we can work with. Execute the command below:

```
Get-ChildItem "<DriveLetter>:\PSLab\Tutorial 7\Groups.txt"
```

The result of the command is shown in Figure 7.0.2.

Figure 7.0.2 - Get-ChildItem properties example

Figure 7.0.2 reveals more properties for this file but there could be more. Let's find out by executing the command below:

```
Get-ChildItem Get-ChildItem
"<DriveLetter>:\PSLab\Tutorial 7\Groups.txt" | Get-Member
```

There are more properties we can work with indeed!. Some notable ones are: Extension, LastWriteTime, Length and Name. The property 'Length' here is different from the 'Length' found in the Get-Content command result.

While the 'Length' in Get-Content told us the number of items in the text file, the 'Length' in Get-ChildItem is the size of the file in Bytes. To determine the size of this file, execute the command below:

```
(Get-ChildItem "<DriveLetter>:\PSLab\Tutorial 7\Groups.txt").Length
```

The command returned 235 as shown in Figure 7.0.3. To confirm that this is the size of the file, see Figure 7.0.4.

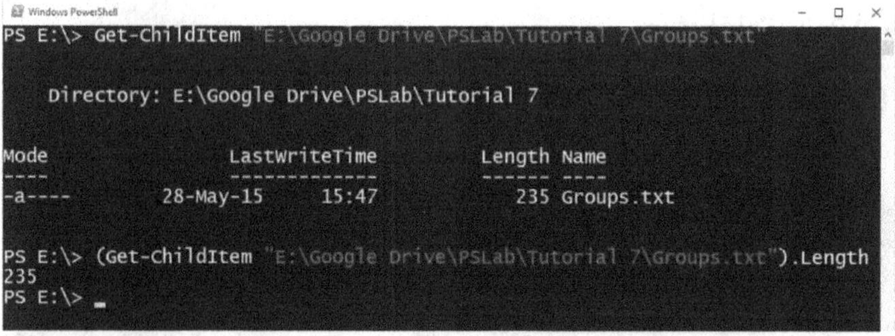

Figure 7.0.3 - Get-ChildItem Length Property

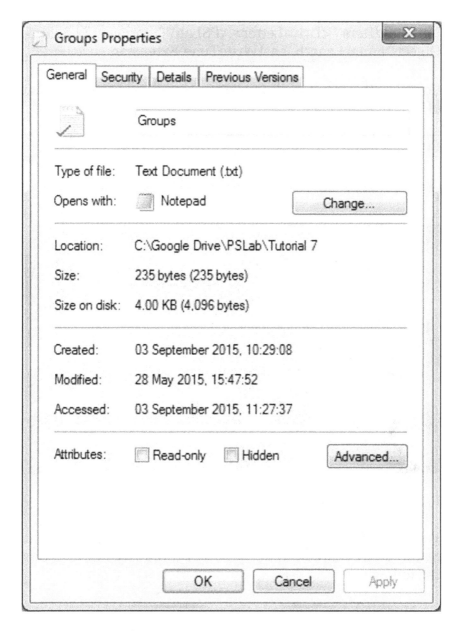

Figure 7.0.4 - File Size

Before we move on from Object Properties, let's determine the Size, Extension and LastWriteTime of all the files located in "<DriveLetter>:\PSLab\Tutorial 7".

```
Get-ChildItem "<DriveLetter>:\PSLab\Tutorial 7\" | Select-
Object Name, Length, LastWriteTime,Extension
```

Compare the result of the previous command with the result of the command below:

```
Get-ChildItem "<DriveLetter>:\PSLab\Tutorial 7\"
```

Output of both commands is shown in Figure 7.0.5.

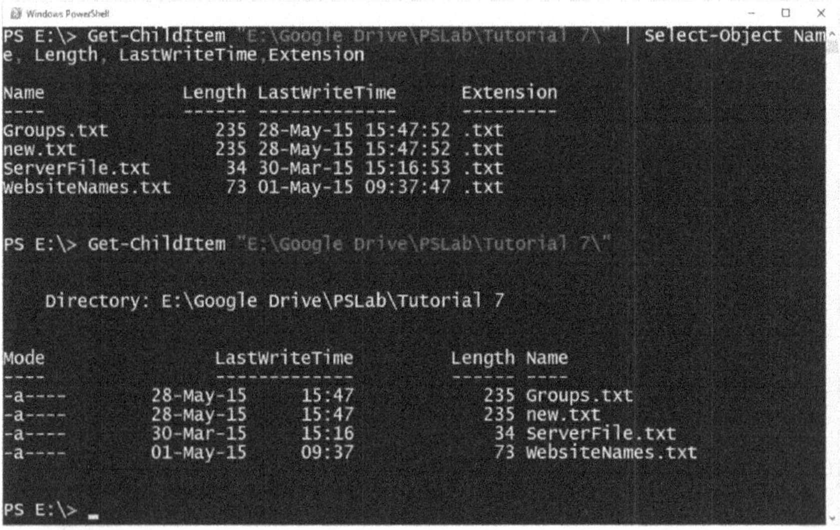

Figure 7.0.5 - Object Properties example

With the first command, we have more control over the result of our command. Let's round off tutorial 7.0 by noting the following:

1. Modified date is exactly the same value as the 'LastWriteTime'. Compare Figures 7.0.4 and 7.0.5.
2. You can combine the information provided by an Object's properties and Logical Operations to achieve a lot in your scripting.
   a. For instance, with 'LastWriteTime' property you can easily delete old files from a folder. Simply pipe the

output of the Get-ChildItem to a Where-Object; specifying that files with specific 'LastWriteTime' should be returned. You can then pipe the result to the Remove-Item command to delete the files.
b. You can also return files of specific Length.

Section Summary

In this section we covered the following:

1. An object is a collection of data that represents an item.
2. An object is made up of three types of data: the objects type, its methods, and its properties.
3. To access the property or method of an object, enclose the object in bracket (), followed by a dot (.) then the property or method.
4. To access a method, additional commands may be required.
5. The object can be stored in a variable and accessed via the variable.
6. The properties or methods of the object can be listed using the following methods:
   a. Get-Member
   b. Command completion
   c. Scripting editor like PowerGUI

7.1 How To Access Object Properties Using Variables

In the last tutorial, you saw how to access an object's properties by enclosing the object (command) in a bracket followed by a dot (.) followed the property you wish to access. When you store the result of a command in a variable, accessing the properties of the object becomes less complicated.

Let's store our last command in a variable called $ObProp:

```
$ObProp  = Get-ChildItem Get-ChildItem
"<DriveLetter>:\PSLab\Tutorial 7\Groups.txt"
```

To access the properties of this object, type the variable name $ObProp, followed by a dot (.) then press the TAB key. The shell will show the properties and methods available for the object stored in the variable. To determine the size of the file, simply execute the command below:

```
$ObProp.Length
```

You can also access the properties of an object using the '$_' automatic variable. To demonstrate this, enter the command below in your PowerShell console and press the TAB key. Again, the shell returns all the properties of the object using the '$_' automatic variable.

```
Get-ChildItem "C:\Google Drive\PSLab\Tutorial
7\Groups.txt" | ForEach-Object {$_.
```

Section Summary

In this section we covered the following:

1. When you store the result of a command in a variable, you can access the properties of the object by adding a dot (.) and pressing the TAB key.
2. You can also access the properties of an object using the '$_' automatic variable.

7.2 Member Types And Applications

In this tutorial, we will examine the different 'MemberTypes' and how you can use them. To proceed, let's execute the Get-ChildItem command:

```
Get-ChildItem Get-ChildItem
"<DriveLetter>:\PSLab\Tutorial 7\Groups.txt" | Get-
Member
```

The result of the command is shown in Figure 7.2.0. The 'MemberType' column has five distinct 'Types' – 'CodeProperty', 'Method', 'NoteProperty', 'Property' and 'ScriptProperty'. We have already defined Method and Property. Below is a definition for the remaining three:

CodeProperty: A code property references a static property of a .NET Framework object.

NoteProperty: A note property defines a property that has a static value.

ScriptProperty: A script property defines a property whose value is the output of a script.

Let's explore the MemberTypes shown in Figure 7.2.0. There is just one MemberType, with the 'CodeProperty' type. The name of this 'CodeProperty' type is 'Mode'.

Figure 7.2.0 - Get-ChildItem, Get-Member for a text file

Let's see the value of CodeProperty, 'Mode'. Execute the command below:

```
(Get-ChildItem "<DriveLetter>:\PSLab\Tutorial
7\Groups.txt").Mode
```

The result of the command returned '-a----'. What does this mean? This value represents the file attributes setting of the text file. '-a----' means that the 'archive' bit is set for this file.

Let's examine this value in the text file. Navigate to the location of the text file, right-click and select Properties. Click 'Advanced' tab. Notice that the *File is ready for archiving* is set? This is why the mode displayed 'a' in the archive portion of the file mode CodeProperty. See Figure

7.2.1.

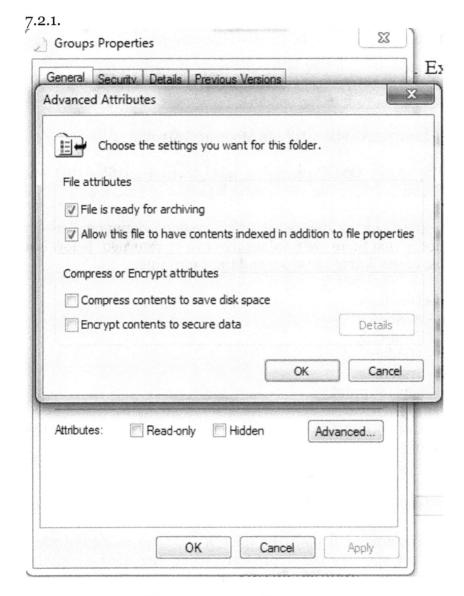

Figure 7.2.1 – Archive setting of a file

Boom! The archive bit is set! If we want to see the meaning of each attribute, we would execute the command below:

```
Get-ChildItem "<DriveLetter>:\PSLab\Tutorial
7\Groups.txt" | Select-Object Mode, Attributes -Unique
```

Figure 7.2.2 shows the result of the command:

Figure 7.2.2 - File attribute Mode and Attributes.

The mode 'CodeProperty' is used to find all files that are "Read Only", or has the archive bit set or are hidden.

Going back to the result of the mode command, '-a----', notice that there are 6 values that can be returned. Below is a list of the potential values and their meaning:

d - Directory
a - Archive
r - Read-only
h - Hidden
s - System
l - Reparse point

To display only the value of the archive attribute, execute the command below:

(Get-ChildItem "<DriveLetter>:\PSLab\Tutorial 7\Groups.txt").Mode[1]

The command displays the value 'a'. You can access the other bits of the Attributes property using the method in the previous command. For example, to return only the 'Directory' attribute 'd', replace '1' with '0' in the previous command.

Object Methods

Refer to Figure 7.2.0. There is a long list of 'Methods' including 'MoveTo', 'CopyTo' and 'Create'. The names of the methods are self-explanatory. To copy the content of

Groups.txt to NewGroups.txt, execute the command nelow:

```
(Get-ChildItem "<DriveLetter>:\PSLab\Tutorial
7\Groups.txt").CopyTo("<DriveLetter>:\PSLab\Tutorial
7\NewGroups.txt")
```

You can apply this to any of the 'Methods'. The examples covered in this tutorial are not exhaustive. I believe you have the knowledge required to work with object Methods. You can play around with the other MemberTypes.

Section Summary

In this section we covered the following:

1. There are five MemberTypes returned by the Get-Member command for a text file using the Get-ChildItem command: CodeProperty, Method, NoteProperty, Property and ScriptProperty
2. Each of the MemberTypes allows you to return or manipulate the properties of the object.
3. The 'Mode' CodeProperty returns the file attributes setting of a text file.

7.3 Exploring The Get-Member Cmdlet

This tutorial will teach you more about the Get-Member cmdlet. You can explore how to use this cmdlet using the Get-Help cmdlet. Let's execute the command below:

```
Get-Help Get-Member -Detailed
```

As usual, the first place to look is the SYNTAX section. We can also find some useful information under the PARAMETERS section. For instance we see that adding the 'Force' parameter includes more MethodTypes that are not displayed by default. This automatically expands the control you have on an object!

We can also return specific MethodTypes. For example, to

return only 'Method' MemberType, execute the command below:

```
Get-Process | Get-Member -MemberType Method
```

If you wish to return 'Properties' MemberType, replace 'Method' with 'Properties' in the previous command.

The Get-Member cmdlet also has an 'InputObject' parameter. This parameter allows you to specify an input object for the Get-Member cmdlet. For example, Get-Process command is the InputObject in the command below:

```
Get-Member -InputObject Get-Process
```

Note

In the previous command, you can store Get-Process in a variable and use the variable as the 'InputObject'.

Section Summary

In this section we covered the following:

1. To get more understanding how to use the Get-Method cmdlet, use *Get-Help Get-Member* with 'Detailed' or 'Full' parameter.
2. You can pipe the out-put of a cmdlet to the Get-Member or use the 'InputObject' parameter.

7.4 How To Use Objects In Pipelines

Some of the things you will learn in this tutorial have already been discussed in passing in previous tutorials. I decided to finish this volume with this final tutorial because of the importance of object properties.

In tutorial 3.4 we discussed pipelines. When commands are combined in a pipeline, the commands pass information to each other as objects.

Let's look at an example:

Get-ChildItem "<DriveLetter>:\PSLab\Tools\ - | Where-Object {$_.PsIsContainer -eq $TRUE} | Format-List

In the command above, Get-ChildItem passed some objects to the Where-Object command. On the other hand, the Where-Object command passed some objects to the Format-List command. The result of the command is shown in Figure 7.2.3

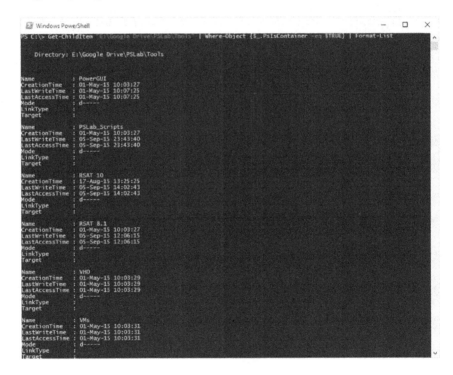

Figure 7.2.3 - Object properties in Pipelines

The previous command returned only folders. All non-folder objects are ignored. Why? The answer is in the 'PsIsContainer' object passed from the Get-ChildItem command. To see this object, pipe the Get-ChildItem command to the Get-Member command.

With the 'PsIsContainer' object passed from the Get-ChildItem command, the Where-Object command is able to specify this object to determine the output of the command. If the 'PsIsContainer' object was not passed from the Get-ChildItem command, trying to access the object will result in an error because it would not exist.

The command also used two concepts we already discussed in previous tutorials. The automatic variables '$_' and '$TRUE'; and the comparison operator 'eq'. In this command, the 'PsIsContainer' property was accessed with the automatic variables '$_', compared with the automatic variables '$TRUE' using the comparison operator 'eq'.

Section Summary

In this section we covered the following:

1. When commands are combined in a pipeline, the commands pass information to each other as objects.
2. The commands in the pipeline are able to use the objects passed to determine the final output of the command.

References And Further Reading

1. About_Objects
   https://msdn.microsoft.com/en-us/library/ms714428%28v=vs.85%29.aspx?f=255&MSPPError=-2147217396
2. About_Properties
   https://technet.microsoft.com/en-us/library/hh847751.aspx
3. About_Methods
   https://technet.microsoft.com/en-us/library/hh847878.aspx
4. About_Object_Creation
   https://technet.microsoft.com/en-us/library/jj159398.aspx
5. Extending Properties for Objects
   https://technet.microsoft.com/en-

us/library/dd878346(v=vs.85).aspx

6. 'Mode' values returned by PowerShell's Get-ChildItem cmdlet?
   http://stackoverflow.com/questions/4939802/what-are-the-possible-mode-values-returned-by-powershells-get-childitem-cmdle

CONCLUSION

Thank you again for buying this book. I hope that you have acquired PowerShell skills from this book "PowerShell Tutorial Volume 1"?

This is the first book in the series. Volume 2 will continue expanding your PowerShell skills. Before you proceed to volume 2, please take time to write a review for this volume on Amazon. Simply share your thoughts and experiences about the book.

To Get information about the other volumes, search "PowerShell Tutorial Volume 2, 3, 4" on Amazon. Alternatively, you can visit the following pages:

Twitter.com/PowerShellDIY
facebook.com/PowerShellTutorialBook
Itechguides.com/PowerShell-Tutorial

If you require help with this book or any other book in this series, please email PSLab@itechguides.com

Other Books By Victor Ashiedu

Hands-On Study Guide for Exam 70-411: Administering Windows Server 2012 R2

POWERSHELL TUTORIAL VOLUME 2: PREVIEW

POWERSHELL TUTORIAL VOLUME 2, the second book in this series has more practical tutorials. This volume moves your PowerShell scripting skills to expert level.

Volume 2 covers more advanced topics. Below is a snippet of the first 2 tutorials covered in Volume 2:

POWERSHELL TUTORIAL 1: Filtering Data Outputs and Results – The first tutorial in Volume 2, teaches how to output specific data from multiple data sources. It covers the use of the Where-Object command to filter data.

Tutorial 1 also teaches how to Format and sort results using the 'Format' Verb cmdlets. It teaches extensive object and data manipulation and much more...

POWERSHELL TUTORIAL 2: Custom Labels and Harsh-Tables – This tutorial teaches how to change object properties to create reports with customized headers. This tutorial also teaches how to create a single report from two or more data sources using Hash Tables.

Tutorial 2 also teaches how to create PSObjects using the New-Object command. Tutorial 2 ends with "Formatting reports".

Continue expanding your PowerShell skills. To be notified when Volume 2 is released, follow the PowerShell Tutorial book series on Facebook:

Facebook.com/PowerShellTutorialBook

ABOUT THE AUTHOR

Victor is a Windows Systems admin with over 13 year's experience. He specializes in Active Directory and automating Windows tasks with PowerShell.

His first book "Hands-on study guide for exam 70-411" is already helping Windows systems administrators learn Windows Server 2012 R2 and pass exam 70-411. He has contributed a number of scripts to the Microsoft script gallery (over 14,000 downloads and counting!).

Victor loves writing and currently works as a Windows Sys Admin. When he is not writing or coding, he visits museums and spends time with his wife. Victor lives in England with his wife Bunmi.

www.ingramcontent.com/pod-product-compliance
Lightning Source LLC
Chambersburg PA
CBHW071158050326
40689CB00011B/2170